How to Prepare a Production Budget for Film & Video Tape

By Sylvia Allen Costa

TAB BOOKS
Blue Ridge Summit, Pa. 17214

FIRST EDITION

FIRST PRINTING—SEPTEMBER 1973

Copyright ©1973 by TAB BOOKS

Printed in the United States
of America

Hardbound Edition: International Standard Book No. 0-8306-3645-5

Library of Congress Card Number: 72-94808

Preface

Budgeting is one of the first steps in the production process. And, once production begins, the budget or estimate is as valuable as the script. Since rates differ across the country, I have not specified exact costs. Instead I have included the necessary questions to ask to determine what rate is applicable for your part of the country and your production. This book is valuable to amateurs as well as professionals. For the student it is a good primer; for the professional, a good reference book.

The author wishes to acknowledge her great indebtedness to the many people who read and offered criticism on the manuscript, especially her husband, John, who insisted that the book be written in the first place.

Special thanks are given to the following people for their invaluable assistance:

Jeffrey Altshuler, Producer, for his research on equipment and opticals;

Mark Dichter, Professor at Columbia and free-lance soundman, consultant on sound and transfers;

Stu Chasmar, President, Bellringer Productions, free-lance consultant on editing;

And special thanks to Glenn Giere, President, The Production Department, for diligently and meticulously editing and correcting the entire manuscript.

Sylvia Allen Costa

Contents

Chapter 1 The Function of an Estimator   7

Breakdown—Equipment Costs—Personnel—Location—Scenic Considerations—Laboratory and Sound Charges—Post Production Costs—Miscellaneous—Overhead—Importance of Estimates

Chapter 2 Studios & Locations   14

Studio Specifications—Charges—Preparing an Estimate—Location Shooting—Budget Checklists

Chapter 3 Equipment   22

Film Equipment—Lighting—Video Tape—Typical Equipment Costs

Chapter 4 Raw Stock   68

Video Tape—Film—Shooting Ratio

Chapter 5 Laboratory Charges   73

Developing—Printing—Final Processes

Chapter 6 Sound Costs   85

Recording—Transfers—Music—Sound Effects—Narration—Mixing

Chapter 7 Production Personnel   92

Technical Personnel—Creative Personnel

Chapter 8 Talent 102

Outside Casting Services—Staff Casting Director—
Agents—Budget Considerations—Do-It-Yourself
Production—Cost Cutting

Chapter 9 Scenic Elements 109

Building a Set—Art Work—Wardrobe—Cue Cards or
Teleprompter—Trucking—Miscellaneous

Chapter 10 Location Expenses 113

Transportation—Food—Lodging—Vehicle Rentals—
Mileage—Shipping—Location-Release Fees—Travel
Time—Miscellaneous

Chapter 11 Survey 118

Location Considerations

Chapter 12 Editing 122

Video Tape—Film Editing—Hiring an Editor

Chapter 13 Opticals & Animation 129

Optical Effects—Animation Stand Photography—
Animation Stand Effects

Chapter 14 Miscellaneous 136

Writer's Fees—Animal Rentals—Special Effects—
Insurance

Chapter 15 Overhead 142

Space—Telephone—Messenger Services—Office Supplies—Administrative & Office Personnel

Chapter 16 Nonunion Production

145

Overhead—Survey—Equipment—Scenic Elements—
Location Expenses—Editing— Technical and Production
Personnel

Chapter 17 Sample Budgets

151

Typical Cost Estimates for Commercials, Documentaries, and a Full-Length 35mm Feature

Glossary

180

Index

191

Chapter 1

The Function of an Estimator

Production estimating is very much like making a patchwork quilt: You must have all the pieces before you can put it together. Many times, inexperienced young filmmakers, and even older professionals, feel that the creative end is more rewarding and more important than the business end. However, in order to keep operating, it is important to be aware of the many cost areas that can be encountered during production. Even if you are not involved in the day-to-day administration of a film production, you should have a working knowledge of these costs to enable you to work more efficiently.

All estimating—feature, commercial, documentary— starts out with the same basic knowledge. However, if you can estimate commercials you have enough knowledge to budget any kind of production, for with commercials you must be totally informed about union personnel, their wage scales and interrelationships, talent, scenic elements, equipment, and other cost areas. Once you know the various elements that go into a production, you just vary the numbers with the type of production you are doing.

BREAKDOWN

An estimator breaks down a script or story treatment in much the same way as a production manager does. To break down the script, he goes through and lists everything needed in each scene on an AD Breakdown Sheet or comparable form. Fig. 1-1 shows an assistant director's breakdown sheet. This list includes all technical equipment and personnel, production personnel, talent, wardrobe, sets, and other scenic elements; in short, all the pieces that must be arranged for and priced out before production can start. Everything is included on this breakdown sheet; nothing is to be left out. This sort of elaborate breakdown is not necessary for all

ASSISTANT DIRECTORS BREAKDOWN SHEET

SEQ. No.

PICT No _____ SET NO: _____ SHEET NO: _____

EXT. _____

INT. | No. | CAST

SCENE

COSTUME No

SCENE NUMBERS

| TOTAL SCENES | TOTAL DIALOGUE | No. PAGES | DAY | NITE |

DESCRIPTION

| PROP S | ATMOSPHERE | BITS |

| CARS — LIVE STOCK | SPECIAL EFFECTS | MUSIC |

Fig. 1-1. Assistant director's breakdown sheet.

productions, but initially, until you become proficient in estimating, this elaborate itemization makes you aware of the many cost areas that are involved in production.

Once the script has been broken down, the estimator must go through it and check every detail. He should discuss the script with the producer and director and from this determine the number of shooting days required and all attendant information for those days. The breakdown should give an exact day-to-day accounting of the script. He then can set up a tentative shooting schedule. This schedule becomes his guideline for arriving at the total production cost.

EQUIPMENT COSTS

Once a tentative schedule has been set up, the estimator must refer again to the breakdown sheets; this time concentrating only on a particular area of the budget, one at a time. After deciding how the project is to be shot—video tape or film, and if film, 16mm, super 16, or 35mm—he can itemize and price the equipment to be used. These figures are totaled and put into the estimate. These are rough figures, and not necessarily to the penny, but close enough to give the producer an approximate idea of equipment costs.

RAW STOCK

After determining his equipment, the next area is raw stock. After determining the shooting ratio, he can then arrive at the estimated amount of video tape stock or film footage needed. Also included in this area is ¼-inch tape for sound recording purposes.

PERSONNEL

In the area of personnel, the filmmaker must first decide if he is going to shoot with a union or nonunion crew. And if a union crew is used he must decide whether his crew should be affiliated with the International Alliance of Theatrical and Stage Employees (IATSE) or the National Association of Broadcast Employees and Technicians (NABET), as that decision, too, will affect his budget. These union interrelationships are discussed in detail in a later chapter. If he is estimating a low-budget production and is not restricted to the New York City area, the estimator would, in all probability, try for a nonunion crew. This way, the fees are not set, overtime is not strictly defined, and the crew can be smaller. However, shooting with a nonunion crew limits the producer to a cinema verité-type production. If the production is to be more elaborate, it is advisable to use a union crew. The union crew must include all technicians, stagehands, directors, assistants, and, when necessary, make-up artists, hairdressers, and wardrobe handlers. When estimating a union production, take into consideration starting times, lunch hours, overtime, and meal penalties, and include them all in your budget.

Depending on the medium being used, there are two performing talent unions to be considered when preparing a budget: Screen Actors Guild (SAG) and American Federation of Television and Radio Artists (AFTRA). Talent is one area where you should always work with union personnel. Even when working with a nonunion crew, always pay union scale for the talent. When budgeting talent, consider casting fees, union pension and welfare contributions, payroll taxes, agents' fees, and other attendant charges as listed in the code books. Many times, talent can be bought for scale; however, if they are well known or in great demand, a fee that is double or triple-scale may have to be negotiated. In the case of a "star," the amount asked for is limitless and the value of their contribution to the filmmaking project must be weighed against the actual expense to determine whether they are essential to the total creative concept.

LOCATIONS / STUDIOS

Depending on the demands of the script, a big cost area can be locations or studios. Where is the production to be shot? Again, be sure to include all costs that can be accrued in a shooting schedule. Find out if fees must be paid to the owner of a certain location, even if the man "promised" you could have free rein with the site. If studios must be rented, find out if they have construction charges, strike charges, what the hours are for a shooting day, if there is a charge for electricity, etc. These must all be totaled and included in the estimate form. Remember that these are just estimated amounts based upon the concept of the producer and-or director, and if the concept or approach changes, so can the budget.

SCENIC CONSIDERATIONS

The area of scenic elements is a large one encompassing the visual aspect of your production. In it are included fees for set designers (art directors) and scenic artists. Included, too, are any scenery and accompanying fixtures such as furniture and smaller props. If special costumes are required, or a stylist needed to choose period pieces, this is all included under this category. Depending on the needs of the production, this area can be quite inexpensive or terribly costly. A cost area to watch out for here is the trucking. This can be astronomical when dealing with union truckers.

LABORATORY AND SOUND CHARGES

If shooting in tape, there are, of course, no laboratory charges. For film, though, these must be figured into the budget. A common practice of some estimators is to lump all raw stock and lab charges together and come up with an average per-foot figure which they use in their budget. This is not as good a system as breaking out each individual area and figuring the exact charges in those areas. Although a budget is merely an estimate of production costs, it should be as accurate as possible. The more detailed the budget is, the less the chance for error. Even include sales tax in the figures where applicable. If you qualify for a resale certificate, you can become exempt from paying sales tax on services and commodities.

If shooting in video tape, sound and transfer charges are not necessary, since the sound is recorded on the video tape. When shooting on film, though, transfer charges must be included, since the ¼-inch tape must be transferred to a medium compatible with the film for editing purposes; i.e., magnetic track. In this area include all additional ¼-inch tape required, time needed to transfer the ¼-inch tape sound to the magnetic track, and the magnetic stock footage. In the chapter on sound we deal with the estimating of time and footage involved.

EDITING

In film there is a basic formula for the editing of a specific production. If it is a half-hour program, you can figure 7 weeks; if an hour, 12 weeks. A commercial should take no longer than 10 days; a feature no longer than 9 months. However, as with everything else, these times can vary with the project. When it comes to editing, take into consideration how many editors and-or assistants are needed, as well as syncing time, equipment, space, and supplies. All these figures should be included in your estimate. If an editing service is to be used, be sure they itemize what they are providing for the price being quoted. Normally, for a commercial it is advisable to use an editing service, since there are very few free-lance editors who are willing to work on as small a project as a commercial. In this area, too, do not forget pension and welfare contributions to the union and payroll taxes where applicable.

There is also a basic formula to use in figuring video tape editing time. Again, as with film, there are exceptions to this rule. As a beginning, though, figure 15 minutes per scene for a simple two-machine edit (one machine in the playback mode and one machine in edit). As the edits become more complicated, the time involved becomes longer. Usually, editing in video tape is a total quote from a production facility and cannot be hired or estimated on an itemized per piece basis as in film.

POST PRODUCTION COSTS

Under the broad category of post production are mixing, opticals, animation and-or graphics, music, answer and release prints. In tape, many of these operations can be done in the studio or during the editing sessions. In film, though, they must be done after the dailies have been edited into a final workprint. When the editor has completed his workprint, it then goes to the optical house and from there to the mix and into the lab for negative cutting and an answer print. It is important that, as an estimator, you know all the steps taken in filmmaking in order to prepare an accurate budget. If the estimator is unfamiliar with any of the steps and does not bother to verify his figures, the estimate can be inaccurate and, in all probability, unworkable. When in doubt, always check with the suppliers involved. They are more than willing to help **before** the production begins rather than having you come back to them after production has begun with a figure that is unrealistic.

MISCELLANEOUS

As with everything else, there must be a miscellaneous category that is the catch-all of the budget. Here the estimator includes all production insurance, errors and omission insurance (when necessary), special equipment, consultant fees, story rights, etc. In other words, everything that is needed to complete the production but for which there is no particular category.

OVERHEAD

Overhead can be handled in one of two ways. The estimator can project how much time will be involved in the project and prorate the filmmaker's facilities and include that as a separate item in the bid. Or, a more common method is to incorporate this figure into the overall production fee. The producer's fee can vary from 5 to 50 percent of the total production cost, depending on the size of the producer's operation. If it is a one-man firm, the fee will be much lower than that of, say, a major production house. Why? There are fewer facilities, less personnel, and, therefore, a much smaller overhead to amortize. There are many things that can affect this percentage and make it vary even more, but the beginning filmmaker should figure 10 to 15 percent of his total below-the-line production cost as a producer's fee.

A brief word about "above-the-line" and "below-the-line." The terminology is used continuously, yet there are varying definitions of them. Basically, below-the-line refers to all physical production costs and above-the-line to those costs incurred in conjunction with the production but not necessary to the actual physical production. Above-the-line refers to legal fees, promotion, accounting, name talent or a name director, original music, and general and administrative services. For the time being it is only important to know what above-the-line refers to and not necessarily how to calculate those figures.

IMPORTANCE OF ESTIMATES

Why do an estimate at all? Why not just go out and shoot your film, and whatever it comes to, that's it? Preparing a budget forces the filmmaker to define exactly what his project is and makes him aware of the many problems and difficulties that can be encountered. A budget is necessary if you intend to get financial backing for your project. No financier will invest in something without first seeing what it costs. It also alerts the filmmaker to some of the "oddities" of the production such as the need for underwater gear, skydiving equipment, mountain-climbing gear, etc. In short, an estimate is a good step towards coordinating your production.

In addition to cost factors, there are human factors that must be taken into consideration when doing an estimate. There are nine unions that you will be dealing with: SAG, AFTRA, AF of M, NABET, IBEW, IATSE, Directors Guild of America (DGA), the Teamsters, and the United Scenic Artists. All have big, thick books that outline working hours, rates, travel time, overtime, golden time, short turn-around, etc., and these are all cost areas that you must know about. Also, some of the unions are not compatible and you must be aware of these relationships, too.

Preparing a budget, then, is not just an exercise in mathematics. It is an attempt to organize the production and give it some perspective. It tells you what it will cost and how long it will take to produce. It is an outline of your filmmaking project.

Chapter 2
Studios & Locations

When preparing an estimate, one of the first things to be determined is the location of the production. Will it be shot in a studio or at an existing site, or a combination of the two? For example, if your production involves a beautiful sunset in the Bahamas or an exciting run down a Vermont ski slope, obviously you will have to work at an actual location, since these conditions cannot be simulated realistically. On the other hand, if you have a scene in a living room, store, or on a street corner, this could be done in a studio. The big advantage to shooting in a studio is control; you can control the lighting, the sound, and the weather, and you can build your set to fit the exact specifications of the script or storyboard.

STUDIO SPECIFICATIONS

Renting a studio is much like renting an apartment or buying a home. There are many little things you should look for and about which you should ask. It is advisable to start a notebook or file containing rental facilities information. In this file or book should be all pertinent information about each studio, such as size, rates, location, etc. Many studios print fact sheets with all the specifications (see Figs. 2-1 and 2-2). However, this is not a general practice, so you must compile your own reference sheets.

CHARGES

How does a studio charge for its facilities? The four main categories are: 1) construction, 2) shooting, 3) cover, and 4) strike. "Construction" refers to the day(s) needed to build and put up your set. "Shooting" refers, of course, to the actual production time. "Cover" is a term used most often in feature shooting and refers to those days that your set is still in the studio but you are out on location. If, during studio shooting, a

LANCE PRODUCTIONS, INC. 353 West 57th Street, New York, N.Y. 10019 Telephone (212) 757-6167

SOUND STAGE

Approx. size 65'x65'x23½'
Cement cyclorama 66'wide x 21' high with 2 compound 6' curves
FREIGHT [353 W. 58th St] sidewalk & 2 freight elevators + 3 self service

ADDITIONAL FACILITIES

4 dressing rooms [air conditioned]
Makeup room
Dark room
DeWalt & Bench saw
16mm projector

EQUIPMENT INCLUDED IN RENTAL

Flats: 4'x10's - 3' x10's - 2' x10's - 1½ x10's - 1' x10's
WORKING KITCHEN SET FOR FOOD COMMERCIALS
Fearless Dolly
6-5M KW spots w/stands
8-2M KW spots w/stands
18-750w spots w/stands
10-inkydinks
2-5M KW Cones w/stands
1-750KW Cone w/stand
1-Fearless & Atlas Boom
2-sets 24 striplights
8-color-tran units
Assorted Grip Stands, Nets, Flags, Silks, various cables

POWER

1200 Amps AC
60 Amps DC
Separate 220 volt camera lines

EXTRA CHARGES FOR

Electric current used
Telephone calls made
Bulbs as they burn out
Tape & other supplies
Fisher Boom
2-4M soft lites
Moviola Crab Dolly
Worrall Geared Head
DeWalt & Bench saws

RATES

Shooting per 8 hr. day: $335.00
Building, Lighting and Striking per 8 hr. day: $195.00
Overtime pro-rata plus $5.00 per hr. for Studio Man

Lessee is responsible for rental of studio once it is booked!

Completely air conditioned, good restaurants nearby, taxis at the door.

Fig. 2-1. Studio specification sheet.

good day comes along when you can shoot your outdoor scenes and you must leave the set up while shooting outside scenes, you are charged for a cover day. If you budget your production properly, there should be very few cover days needed in your estimate. "Strike" refers to the time needed to take the set down and clean up the studio. In most cases, construction and strike days are cheaper than cover and shooting days.

One of the most important considerations concerns the official studio hours. What are they? Are the hours rigid or flexible? Most union studios operate between 8:30 AM and 5:30

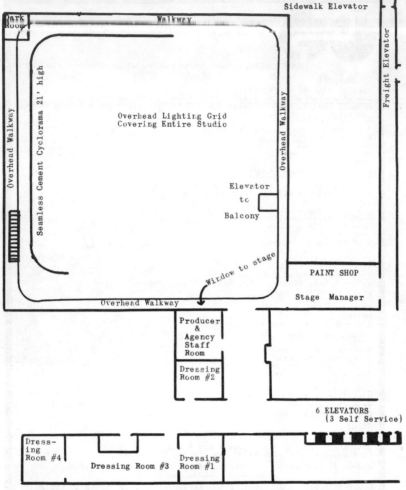

Fig. 2-2. Studio layout sheet.

PM Monday through Friday. Any time within those hours is charged at the regular daily rate. All other times, including Saturday, Sunday, and legal holidays, are considered overtime. Be sure to get the overtime rates for all categories. For example, if you are scheduled to shoot from 9:30 AM to 6:30 PM on a week day, even though you have used only a regular 8-hour day, you are charged for a regular day plus one hour of overtime because you went past the 5:30 PM cutoff. Once you know the operating hours of the studio you are using, production costs can be cut by scheduling your day within those hours.

In addition to the rental rates, you are also charged a flat fee for electricity, telephone use on a flat fee or per-time basis, and any purchase or rental of bulbs. The electrical fee is higher on shooting days than on construction, strike, or cover days. Check, too, to see if you are billed for any local taxes that are paid by the stage owner. In New York, for example, a small percentage of the occupancy tax is paid by each studio rentee. Find out what insurance they carry, if you are charged for it, and what insurance you must have. If the stage is not left in a clean condition, there may be a clean-up charge and a rubbish removal charge.

PREPARING AN ESTIMATE

What information must you have about studios to prepare an estimate accurately? Find out the size of the studio, including the height. A car commercial would not be shot in the same size studio as one used for a shampoo. How accessible is it? If it is not on the ground floor, do they have a service elevator and, if there is an elevator, how big is it? This information is necessary, since the studio is of no value to you if the elevator is not big enough to accommodate your sets, props, and equipment.

What type of power supply is available? Does the stage come with a complete complement of lights? Is it cheaper to buy or rent the bulbs? Are the bulbs new ones? Are they dark and ready to go? If not, replacement of the bulbs can be very expensive. Does it have a grid system and is any grip (barn doors, sand bags, appleboxes, etc.) equipment included in the rental? Is it a film studio or video tape, or both?

Does it have a cyc? (Short for cyclorama; refers to a smooth piece of material stretched taut and used as background to give a feeling of infinity. Made of material, no-seam paper, or in some stages it is solid.) Is the cyc a permanent one? If so, the size of the stage is reduced and may prohibit the building of certain sets. Conversely, if your script calls for a neutral background, the studio with the permanent cyc becomes the ideal stage for your production. Most studios with a permanent cyc are responsible for maintaining it in a good state of white. If you want some color other than white, you will be charged for both painting the cyc the color you want and restoring it to its original white. This can be a very expensive paint job, because it may take two coats of paint to cover a dark color. By closely studying your script or storyboard prior to production, you can determine the right stage or studio to meet the production needs and save money as well as unnecessary production headaches.

Does the studio have adequate dressing room facilities? Are they clean? Are there facilities for make-up, wardrobe and hair? Does it have a working kitchen? Is there a shop area where sets can be constructed? Or will the sets have to be built outside and trucked in. Are the loading and unloading facilities adequate? Enough rest rooms? What overnight security do they provide? Will you need to hire a guard to protect props and equipment?

An important question to resolve with each studio is one involving unions. Does the studio have a signed contract with any union? If so, find out which one. If you take a rival union into a studio where a competing union holds a contract, there will be a work stoppage. At one time almost all studios were signed to a union contract. However, with the growth of NABET (National Association of Broadcast Employees and Technicians) and the trend toward nonunion production, these studios are numbering fewer each year. Don't assume they do or do not have a signed contract. Always find out before going into production.

LOCATION SHOOTING

Anything shot outside of a studio is considered location shooting or a remote. Location shooting can affect your overall budget in the area of personnel because some unions pay time and a half for any remote work. Be sure you totally understand the rules and regulations of all the unions before preparing an estimate and before going into full production. It can save time and money.

Location charges are not as easily defined as those for studios. Sometimes they are free; at other times the charges are exorbitant, but all are negotiable. After deciding upon a location and determining the charge, if the fee is too high it might be cheaper to consider building a set and shooting in a studio if it can be done without a loss of creativity.

If you are going to shoot in an area that is familiar to you, do your own location scouting. However, if you are going into an area that you do not know or if you are pressed for time, there are specific location scouting services. If such a service is used, be sure to include their fee in the production estimate as well as the fee to the location. Although these services are good, often location scouting becomes a matter of "winging" it. Many times the yellow-page section of the telephone book is as good a source of locations as any.

When deciding on a location, there are many things to consider beside price. Is the location accessible? Will transportation have to be arranged for all personnel to and from the site? Are you close to eating facilities or will it be necessary to have the meals catered? Is the available power supply suitable? Is it sufficient or will you have to bring a generator? If your equipment breaks down, do you have easy access to additional equipment or should you budget backup equipment in your estimate? All of these items can affect the total production cost.

Will you need wardrobe vans as well as make-up trucks and dressing room facilities? Will portable sanitation units have to be included in your budget? Is there access to a telephone or should you budget a mobile phone? Is food involved in the production? If so, is there a place for the home economist to work?

Are there any neighborhood restrictions? Do you need a location permit? To find out if a permit is necessary, contact the local Chamber of Commerce in the area where you intend to shoot. If there is a charge for the permit, be sure to include it in the estimate.

Are you shooting in a heavy traffic area? Will you need policemen to help direct traffic? If the police department is notified in advance, they will help during production. This includes directing traffic, posting "no parking" signs, and keeping pedestrians out of the shooting area.

Once a price has been agreed upon and the location committed, it is advisable to have a location release signed (Fig. 2-3). The release serves a two-fold purpose. First, it acts as a binding agreement between you and the property owner. Second, it relieves the producer of any liability as a result of using the premises for the production or any subsequent lawsuits that might arise from use of the location.

Just a reminder at this point that if the location is quite remote, per diem charges must be included in the budget. In general, these cover transportation, food, and lodging for all personnel involved, including talent. Also included in these figures are travel time and mileage, where applicable. These will be discussed in detail in Chapter 11.

BUDGET CHECKLISTS

In summary, answer as many of the following questions as possible before making a commitment to a studio. The answers to these questions will determine whether or not it is feasible to use that particular studio for your production.

a. What are the studio measurements (length, width, height)?

LOCATION RELEASE

Permission is hereby granted to (Producer) to use the property
located at _____
consisting of _____
for the purpose of photographing and recording scenes for the motion
picture tentatively entitled _____.
Said permission shall include the right to bring personnel and
equipment (including props and temporary sets) onto said property and
to remove the same therefrom after completion of work. The permission
herein granted shall include the right, but not the obligation, to
photograph the actual name connected with the premises and to use
such name in the pictures, but(Producer) shall at its election use
another name for the purpose of its picture. Should (Producer) find it
necessary to depict the interior of the above named premises, the
undersigned acknowledge and agrees that (Producer) shall not be required
to depict said interior in any particular manner in connection with the
scenes which it may photograph for its picture.

The above permission granted for one or more days as may be necessary
for _____ commencing on or about
(subject to change in case of changes in the production schedule or
weather conditions), and continuing until completion of all scenes
required. No charge is to be made except for days on which the afore-
said property is actually used for photography.

(Producer) hereby agrres to hold the undersigned harmless of and from
any and all liability and loss which the undersigned may suffer or
incur by reason of any to or death of any person, or damage to
any property, caused by any of its employees or equipment on or about
the above mentioned premises.

The undersigned does hereby warrant and represent that the undersigned
has (have) full right and authority to enter into this agreement concerning
the above described premises, and that the consent or permission of
no other person, firm or corporation is necessary in order to enable
hereinabove described, and the undersigned does (do) hereby indemnify
and agrres to hold (Producer) free and harmless from and against any
and all loss costs, liability, damages or claims or any nature arising
from growing out of or concerning a breach of the above warrantly.

(PRODUCER) PRODUCTION #_____ NAME_____

PRODUCT_____

A.D._____ADDRESS_____

Fig. 2-3. Location release form.

b. What are the operating hours?
c. What are the rates for construction, shooting, cover, and strike days?
d. Overtime rates applicable?
e. Are there additional charges such as electricity, telephone, insurance, bulbs, taxes?
f. What floor is the studio on?

g. Freight elevator? Size?

h. Are there adequate loading and unloading facilities?

i. What equipment is included in the rental price?

j. Do they have a signed contract with a union? Which one?

k. What power supply is available?

l. Does it have a cyc? Is it permanent?

m. Is there a working kitchen?

n. Are there sufficient dressing room, wardrobe, make-up, and hair facilities?

o. Is there a shop area for set construction?

p. Are there sufficient rest rooms?

q. Film, video tape or both?

For locations the following questions are pertinent to preparing an accurate estimate.

a. What is the fee for the location?

b. Is it accessible?

c. Is a permit required? What does it cost?

d. What power supply is available?

e. Do you need wardrobe, make-up and hair vans? Portable dressing rooms?

f. Are portable sanitation units needed?

g. Telephones?

h. Is food preparation involved in the production? Where will the home economist work?

i. What are the neighborhood restrictions?

j. Is the location release signed?

k. Are there public eating facilities nearby or will food have to be provided for the cast and crew?

l. Will policemen be necessary during production?

m. Is the shooting area so remote that backup equipment must be brought along in case of equipment breakdown?

n. Union rates for location shooting considered?

These questions will serve not only as budgeting checklists, but also checklists for production. By attempting to answer as many of these questions as possible, your budget will be quite accurate.

Chapter 3
Equipment

When you begin budgeting equipment, you will have already decided on the production medium to be used. The two major forms are, of course, film and video tape. In film, the three subheadings are 35mm, 16mm and Super 16. Your equipment costs are determined by the time of day (or night), location (studio or remote), mobility of production, sync sound, equipment portability, etc. In short, the total specifications used to outline the physical characteristics of your production pertain, too, to equipment. The equipment needed for a film or video tape production falls into five main categories:

1. Camera and accessories
2. Sound
3. Lighting
4. Grip
5. Miscellaneous

FILM EQUIPMENT

Certain characteristics germane to the various types of filmmaking make it possible to develop some generalities about budgeting equipment. When shooting a feature or commercial, there is usually a carefully detailed script or storyboard from which to work. The intricate moods and variety of shots found in features and commercials often dictate complicated and elaborate camera and lighting setups. And, since the production is usually well detailed, the cost of each piece of equipment can be accurately budgeted, according to its function and the duration of time it will be needed. In the past, most of this shooting was done in studios where conditions were controlled and equipment easily accessible. Now, however, with the trend toward location shooting, a large item in any production budget becomes trucking, since all equipment, such as lights, cameras, dollies, cranes, and generators, usually found in the studio, must now be taken to the location if the same studio production standards are to be met. Since these productions demand a high film resolution for projection purposes, they are usually done in 35mm.

On the other hand, documentaries and industrials are not as well defined and are less complicated in their production needs. These are usually shot on location, cinema verité style, without a script. The equipment must be portable and adaptable to surroundings not specifically designed for filming. Usually, these productions are shot in 16mm because the equipment is light and compact and allows you greater mobility. Lighting, too, is less complicated, since its major function is to illuminate, not create an effect. The lightweight, portable equipment used in documentaries and industrials is usually battery powered, thereby eliminating the need for bulky generators.

Documentaries and industrials can also be shot in Super 16. By enlarging the aperture on the film gate in the camera, you get a 20 percent greater image, in the same aspect ratio as 35mm, which allows the film to be blown up to 35mm and still retain good resolution and clarity of picture. This means that although the film will be released in 35mm, all the production advantages of 16mm can be utilized. With the equipment adapted to Super 16, you can effect savings of as much as 50 percent on equipment rentals, raw stock, lab charges, and optical printing.

When preparing your budget, remember that location shooting is sometimes more involved than studio shooting, 16mm or 35mm. A studio offers a controlled environment—no weather conditions to worry about, controlled light and sound, proper power supply, backup equipment, etc. For location shooting, though, you must budget weather days, additional lights and reflectors for changing light conditions, a generator to operate the electrical equipment, extra batteries for the camera and tape recorder, wind screens for the microphones, extra lenses, and backup camera and sound equipment, in case of a malfunction during production. All these charges are to be included in your budget.

Cameras & Accessories

The camera is the main piece of equipment in your production. The choice of camera and accessories depends on the shots indicated in your script or storyboard. In a large production it is advisable for the director, cameraman and producer to decide on the type of camera to be used. The director and cameraman make their decisions from a creative point of view; the producer must be sure that their creative decisions are in line with the budget.

Without going deeply into technical specifications, it is helpful to have some knowledge of the cameras available as well as their suitability to different productions. In 35mm feature and commercial production, the most widely used camera for both studio and location shooting is the Mitchell BNC. This is a "self-blimped" camera. A camera that is self-blimped is insulated against noise when it is manufactured and is used for shooting synchronous sound. For cameras not self-blimped, a casing (or blimp) can be rented separately. The blimp hides the operating noise of the camera during sound takes. However, it also makes it bulkier, and functions, such as focusing and magazine loading, take longer, which adds to production time. If only a small portion of your production is sync sound, estimate the cost of the blimp only for the time required. If most of your production is sync sound, it is advisable to rent a self-blimped camera because it is easier to work with. Both Mitchell and Arriflex have developed lightweight, easy-to-handle, self-blimped 35mm cameras. These are the Mitchell Mark III and the Arriflex 35BL.

For silent shooting (m.o.s), the Arriflex 35-2C series is most often used. It is easy to set up and move around and, when blimped, is still light enough for hand-held sync sound use with the aid of a body trace. Blimping approximately doubles the rental price of the camera. The 16mm Arriflex S and M models are also used for m.o.s. shooting and may be blimped for sound shooting. The 16 S accepts 100-foot daylight spools internally and 200- and 400-foot magazines externally. The 16 M has no internal film capacity, but takes 200-, 400-, and 1200-foot magazines.

Another popular camera for m.o.s. shooting is the Eclair CM3. This lightweight, hand-held camera is especially useful where continuous shooting is required because the magazine can be changed in 5 seconds. One variation of this camera is convertible from 35mm to 16mm. This camera, too, can be blimped.

With 16mm documentaries and industrials, the cameras most often used are the Eclair and Arriflex series. Usually, these cameras are self-blimped and can be adapted to shoot cordless sync. The Eclair ACL is the smallest camera and is so lightweight that it rests on the cameraman's shoulder, leaving both hands free to focus and zoom. This is an exceptionally good camera for tight places and limited shooting areas.

There are two ways of recording sync sound: "double" system and "single" system. In a double system, the camera records the picture and a separate sound recorder records the sound. A synchronizing device between the camera and recorder assures that no speed variation exists between the two. In single-system shooting, the sound is recorded simultaneously in the camera on the same film as the picture. This way the picture and sound are combined and ready to project the minute the film has been processed. Newsreel photography is usually shot in 16mm with single-system sound. This allows for last-minute delivery of a story for newscast purposes without spending time syncing the sound with the picture. This system is not practical for other types of shooting, since it is difficult to edit and the sound quality is poor. Auricon makes the most popular series of single-system cameras. The Arriflex 16BL series can also be modified to shoot single-system sound.

For Super 16, standard 16mm cameras in which the aperture gate has been modified are used. The most common one is the Eclair NPR.

Each camera, 16mm and 35mm, comes with two to four magazines to hold the film load. If extensive shooting is to be done, it is advisable to rent extra magazines. The standard sizes in 35mm are 400- and 1000-foot loads; in 16mm, 400-foot loads are common. However, 200- and 1200-foot magazines are available, depending upon the size of the camera.

Regardless of whether you are shooting in 16mm or 35mm, there are some accessories that are basic to both types of camera setups. When shooting, the camera may be hand-held, mounted on a tripod, or on a dolly. If hand-held, you may need a shoulder pod. The tripod is a stationary support with a "head" upon which the camera rests. The head is movable and allows the camera to pan from side to side and up and down. Another form of tripod is the "hi-hat," a short mount that can be placed on a table or on the floor for a low-angle shot. Tripods are rented on a daily or weekly basis.

The type of dolly needed depends on the camera moves—forward, backward, diagonal, raising, and lowering. The crab dolly performs all of these functions and is the most frequently used. If the camera moves are to be tightly controlled, a track must be laid. You would then use a "spyder" dolly. Track is rented on a per foot or per section basis; the dollies on a daily or weekly basis.

Although insignificant as cost factors, the slate and changing bag are two items necessary for any camera setup.

The slate provides a means of identifying each production scene and synchronizing the start of the camera and recorder. The changing bag allows the magazines to be loaded and unloaded without a darkroom.

When preparing your estimate, consider power sources and the power needed to run the camera and other equipment. Professional studios usually have sufficient power. The type of power needed, of course, depends on the equipment being used. Batteries are available in 6-, 8-, 12- and 16-volt sizes. Generators of all sizes are available for heavier equipment. Incidentally, the power supply referred to is for cameras, sound equipment and lights, so be sure you have enough. If batteries are used, budget extra batteries and a charger to guarantee an ample power supply.

When budgeting optics it is essential to know the specific lenses and filters needed. Basic camera rental prices usually include three lenses with fixed focal lengths. With the widespread use of the zoom lens, some equipment rental houses will substitute a zoom lens for all of the fixed-length lenses. This can be quite a savings when compared to renting the zoom separately. The zoom lens is important in documentary and industrial filming, since it allows a great choice of focal lengths, from wide-angle to telephoto, without taking time to change lenses. One lens can be used for an entire production. There are other optics available—fisheye lenses, anamorphic lenses, telephoto lenses, dyna lenses, special effects filters, and prisms. Standard color density filters complete the basic optics requirement. These are rented on a daily or weekly basis or, at times, purchased.

Sound Recording

Sound for film is recorded either in sync with the camera or "wild" (sound effects, narration, room tone, voice-overs, etc.). When sound must be recorded in synchronization with the picture, a means must be provided to insure that both camera and recorder run at the same speed or, if this is not practical, a means must be provided to "resolve" the speed of one during playback to match the speed of the other. This second method is the one most often used today.

The old studio method of recording sync sound was to use sprocketed magnetic film, which was electrically interlocked to the camera and operated at the same speed. The recording machines for this were quite large and cumbersome. Now, virtually all sound recording for film is done on ¼-inch magnetic tape and transferred later to magnetic film for editing purposes. The ¼-inch recorders are light, compact and very portable, making them equally usable in the studio and on location.

Standard camera speed, whether 16mm or 35mm, is 24 frames per second. Standard speed for the sound recorder is 7½ inches per second (i.p.s.). When filming in a location where commercial power is available, the 60-cycle frequency of the commercial power becomes the synchronizing signal, which controls the speed of the camera and is recorded on the sound track as a "sync" signal.

When commercial power is not available, the camera and recorder each run on their own set of batteries. In this instance, a tiny "sync" generator in the camera generates a signal that varies in frequency with any variation of camera speed. This signal is carried by a "sync cable" to the recorder where it is recorded on the sound track. If it is not practical to run a cable between the camera and recorder, the signal can be "broadcast" from a small transmitter on the camera to a small receiver on the recorder. A more recent method that eliminates any signal between camera and recorder is "crystal sync." The camera speed is controlled precisely by a tiny crystal oscillator, and a duplicate oscillator in or at the recorder generates the sync signal which is recorded on the sound track. This system is quite precise but also quite expensive to rent.

Regardless of which means you use to produce the sync signal, when the sound track is transferred to magnetic film the sync signal is fed through an electronic device called a "resolver" which minutely varies the speed of the playback machine to match any variation in the speed of the camera. If, when filming, the camera slows down to 23 f.p.s. or speeds up to 25, the sync signal will vary also. The resolver will sense this change and vary the speed of the playback machine accordingly. Thus, the magnetic film containing the sound track will also have the same minute speed variations as the camera, and both film and track will be in perfect sync.

The prime requirement for a machine to record sync sound is that it be able to run at a constant speed, be of good fidelity, and be equipped to pick up a sync signal from the camera. The signal, which is recorded on the ¼-inch tape, varies as the camera speed varies but has no effect on recorder speed. The recorder should also be equipped with such features as fast forward and rewind, and various monitoring devices for the sync pulse and playback. The Nagra series of recorders are the most widely used for sync sound recording. Other manufacturers are Uher, Tandberg, and Stellavox.

The only requirement for a recorder to take "wild" sound is that the quality of reproduction must be commensurate with your production purposes. Recorders not equipped for sync sound generally rent for about half the cost of sync recorders. Nagra, Uher, Tandberg, and Stellavox also make recorders for taking "wild" sound.

When camera and recorder are connected by cable for sync sound, you must have a recorder for each camera shooting at the same time, unless you have crystal control sync, which allows multiple cameras to be used with one recorder.

While most recorders are supplied with standard microphones, it is generally necessary to obtain separate microphones to suit your particular production. The necessary mike selection is best determined by your soundman (he may have a preference in recorders, too). The type of microphone most often used in recording sync sound is the unidirectional microphone. This mike is aimed in the direction of the source being recorded and picks up a minimum of sound from any other direction. Special ultra-directional microphones, known as "shot-gun" mikes, have an even narrower pickup field. Omnidirectional microphones pick up sound from all sides. These are generally used to record crowds or groups from a central position, and to pick up room tone and sound effects.

Lavalier mikes are worn around the neck and often can be concealed under a piece of clothing. These are especially useful when the subject must move around a great deal, where it would be difficult to be followed by a boom, or where there is a long shot that would expose a hanging or boom mike. When movement or long shots that cover large areas would possibly expose the cable, you might need a wireless mike. In this case, the recorder is connected to a receiver and the performer wears a small transmitter. The Sennheiser series of microphones have the greatest variety of mikes from which to choose and are the most widely used in film production. These are rented on a daily or weekly basis.

When not worn around the neck or held by hand directly in front of a subject, the mike must be suspended out of the frame of the picture but close enough to the subject's mouth to pick up the sound with good quality. The simplest method is to hang a stationary microphone from a grip stand or from a "fish-pole." A fishpole is simply a long sectioned pole, supported on a stand or held by hand. If movement is needed, hang your mike on a "boom." A boom can move around 360 degrees and can telescope, move sideways, forward or back. The base of the boom is on wheels for mobility. Often the movement of the mike and boom must be planned as carefully and thoroughly as the action to be filmed. When using two or more mikes to one recorder, a "mixer" is used to balance the volume of the mikes.

Most recorders and microphones operate on batteries which are included in the rental, although a spare set is a good idea. You should always specify whether you are planning AC or battery operation. The necessary cables are included in the rental price, but extra cables, as well as other accessories (windscreens, amplifiers, etc.), are charged for separately. Be sure to specify the type of camera and recorder being used because cable plugs can vary in size.

LIGHTING

Lighting serves two purposes. The first function is essential—to illuminate the subject being photographed; the second is creative—to set the visual mood of the scene. Although you can estimate the basic lighting needs of your production, it is advisable to consult with your director of photography and-or lighting director if any particular lighting effects are needed. Each unit is selected on the basis of wattage, color temperature, and intensity according to its lighting function in the production. If you are shooting on location, size and weight, too, must be taken into consideration.

The following items are included under lighting equipment: a) lights, b) bulbs, c) means of support (stands, etc.), d) power supply, and e) lighting accessories (grip equipment).

Lighting is applied either directly or indirectly. Direct lighting means the light is thrown directly on the subject. This type of lighting is used in newsreel, documentary, and industrial filming. There are many types of lights available for this type of shooting, including spotlights, floodlights, "broads" (lights that floodlight a large area), "sun guns" (hand-held battery-powered quartz lights), and cyc strips. Fresnel lenses can be added to magnify and intensify the lights.

With indirect lighting, the light source is shielded and provides uniform reflected illumination which is softer. Cone lights and soft lights are indirect. This type of lighting is used in commercial and feature productions. Since there are more lights and the production mood more difficult to achieve, setup time is longer for indirect lighting.

Lighting units must be mounted. In a studio, this can be done on the ceiling grids and on stands. On location, stands and sometimes scaffolding are used. Stands are available in several sizes, according to the size of the unit to be supported, and usually are included in the light rental price. Bulbs, cable, power accessories, and grip equipment are extra cost factors. These can be rented individually or in kits (prepared lighting units that have 2 to 6 light heads, cables, stands, and carrying cases).

Light heads vary in strength from 150 to 10,000 watts. Generally, the greater the bulb strength the greater the expense. Mole-Richardson, Colortran, Century, and Lowell are the better known manufacturers of lighting equipment.

Bulbs must be rented or purchased to use in the light heads. The most often used are the quartz (tungsten-halogen) lamps. Quartz bulbs are lighter than incandescent lamps and smaller. They also burn longer and cleaner with no loss of intensity or color temperature during the life of the bulb. Quartz lamps have less filament "sing" than incandescent lamps. This noise, produced by the vibration of the filament, can be picked up by the sound equipment and ruin your take. Whether rented or purchased, it is advisable to include some extra bulbs in case of burnout or breakage.

Power and power-related equipment is an important consideration in budgeting lighting equipment. As discussed earlier, most studios have sufficient power. Some items to be aware of, many of which are **not** included in the studio rental, are electricity, extra cables, special plugs, voltage regulators to maintain consistent current, switches, adapters, plugging boxes for multiple outlets, and dimmers or dimmer boxes.

On location, a generator is used to power the lighting equipment (as well as cameras, etc.). If the lighting setup is small, a portable generator is sufficient. For heavier lighting and camera setups, large truck-mounted generators must be used. In addition to the generator rental charges, there are gasoline and mileage charges as well as additional manpower to drive and operate the generator.

Grip equipment is the catchall for miscellaneous equipment used in production. "Barn doors" (shutters mounted on lights that allow the light direction to be changed); filters and gels that affect the color of the light; "cookies," flags, scrims (other ways of shielding or shadowing the light beam); reflectors, etc., are all part of grip equipment. Sandbags, "apple boxes," masking tape, etc., are also included in this category.

Under "miscellaneous" goes any unusual or one-time-only equipment. Included are fancy lenses, special camera mounts, customized equipment, and cranes. A high-speed motor might be needed to shoot slow motion. If a high overall shot is needed, you might need to rent a crane. The most popular is the Chapman or Houston "Fearless." These are very large and have platforms for the camera and cameraman. This platform can be raised many feet to permit a high overall shot. Since it is larger, the trucking expenses are high and at least two additional crewmen are needed to operate it, which also adds to your budget. Sometimes special equipment can be rented, such as the cranes; other times, if it is too highly specialized, it must be purchased and the full cost included in your budget, since its use is limited to your particular production.

VIDEO TAPE

In film, the camera transfers the picture directly to the film raw stock and is simply an optical transporter of the visual image. In video tape, the camera transports the image electronically and the video tape recorder (VTR) stores the information on tape in electronic form, in the same way ¼-inch tape is recorded. Thus, in tape, two pieces of equipment provide the basic setup. And, unlike film that needs a second instrument for sound, in video tape the sound is recorded by the same machine as the picture and is stored on the same medium. Lighting for film and tape is similar, although sometimes tape requires higher intensity lights than film. Tape uses the same lighting accessories and grip equipment as film.

The major manufacturers of video tape equipment are Ampex, Marconi, Norelco, and RCA. A basic video tape setup consists of one camera and one VTR. The standard VTR is the Ampex 2000 which can handle 90 minutes of continuous video tape. The camera most widely used is the Norelco PC 70. Another popular camera is the Marconi. For hand-held or location shooting either the Norelco PCP 70 or PCP 90 are used. These cameras operate on batteries and are used in conjunction with the AVR 3000, a small VTR manufactured by Ampex that accepts 20-minute reels of tape and also operates on batteries. Video tape cameras are more restricted than film as to the types of lenses they can use.

If multiple cameras are used, a switcher must be included in your estimate. The switcher allows you to select the desired camera signal to record, as well as adding optical effects such as wipes, dissolves, split screen, etc. With a switcher, the director can decide at the moment of recording which camera to use at any given moment. If you wish to save all the material recorded by each camera, you will need one VTR per camera. It is possible to have any combination of cameras and VTRs you wish, depending on your production needs. This equipment is available for studio rentals or in mobile trucks. These trucks, equipped especially for location shooting, have cameras, switchers, VTRs, and generators for power and are rented on a daily, weekly or monthly basis.

Since most video tape equipment is electronic, power is important. The cameras, VTRs, and other accessory equipment require much electricity to operate. Therefore, the studio must be equipped to handle a large draw of operating power. On location, large generators are usually necessary. As with film, include cabling and voltage regulators in your budget.

Unlike film, video tape equipment cannot be rented on a piece-by-piece basis. Usually, equipment is obtained from a facilities house (i.e., full production setups that rent their facilities to independent productions) or your local TV station. In most cases this is a package deal that includes equipment, studio or mobile unit, and crew. If you are not experienced in estimating video tape costs, the company renting the equipment will be able to help you determine the number of men, equipment, etc.

The prices to be included in your budget can be determined a number of ways. If your production is long (over 10 weeks) consider buying your equipment instead of renting it. For shorter productions, ask for a frequency discount. It can be as much as 20 percent on weekly rentals and 35 percent on monthly. Also, be sure to include any trucking pickup and delivery charges in your budget. Usually rentals are only charged Monday through Friday, so if you take any equipment Friday morning and return it Monday evening, you are only charged for 2 days, even though you may have used it all weekend.

Budgeting equipment takes some knowledge of the production result wanted. When preparing your estimate, consult with the lighting director, soundman, director of photography, director, and producer. If your production is small and you are performing all of these functions, get advice from an equipment rental house or local TV station. The advice is free and invaluable. Don't try to guess what equipment is needed; if you do, you will probably lose production time and production quality.

Equipment, then, includes cameras and accessories (film and video tape), sound equipment, including tape recorders and microphones (film and video tape), VTRs and switchers (video tape), lights and complementary lighting equipment, grip equipment, and specialized equipment such as cranes, underwater housings, etc. (film and video tape). If you determine the exact amount of equipment and the actual time it will be needed for your production, your estimate will accurately reflect the total equipment charges for your particular production. Following are excerpts from a rental catalog offered by F & B / CECO, Inc., New York.

GENERAL RENTING PROCEDURE

1. Reserve your equipment well in advance. Since all rentals are thoroughly checked before leaving our premises, you will avoid delay by giving us prior notice.

2. You are invited to check and inspect the equipment before taking it out.

3. Any rental returned after 10:00 A.M. will be charged rent for that day.

4. All rentals shipped out of the New York City area are two days minimum.

5. Travel allowance of one day at no charge for rental beyond 300 mile radius of New York City. We suggest shipping via Air Freight except in short distance areas.

6. There is no additional charge for fibre packing and carrying cases where practical. Wood crating available at nominal charge.

7. For your own protection, we recommend that you insure all equipment before it leaves our premises.

8. All rentals are subject to a deposit unless an open account has been established with our Credit Department. New customers should submit a credit application at least two weeks prior to the first rental.

(Complete rental regulations will be found on the back of each rental contract.)

ALL PRICES AND/OR SPECIFICATIONS
ARE SUBJECT TO CHANGE WITHOUT NOTICE

F&B/CECO PELLICLE REFLEX BNC CAMERA
with 25, 50, 75mm lenses, viewfinder, 4-1000'
magazines 110v or 220v sync motor 165.00

F&B/CECO PELLICLE REFLEX BNC CAMERA
with 20/120 varifocal lens, 4-1000'
magazines 110v or 220v sync motor 200.00

MITCHELL BNCR CAMERA
with 25, 50, 75mm lenses, viewfinder, 4-1000'
magazines 110v or 220v sync motor 165.00

F&B/CECO VTR REFLEX BNC CAMERA
with Sony vidicon camera and electronic viewfinder
mounted on BNC door. Video image taken off BNC
lens while filming. Can be video taped or used with
monitor only, for remote viewing. BNC with 25, 50,
75mm lenses, 4-1000' magazines, 110v or 220v
sync motor 190.00
above with video recorder and 9" monitor 250.00

TECHNISCOPE REFLEX BNC CAMERA
with 25, 50, 75mm lenses, viewfinder, 4-1000'
magazines, 110v or 220v sync motor 200.00

ADDITIONAL REFLEX BNC LENSES
8mm f2.8 Fisheye 25.00
15mm to 150mm lenses 15.00
Angenieux 20-120mm zoom lens 80.00
Canon 25-120mm Macro zoom lens 75.00
Angenieux 25-250mm zoom lens 55.00
40-400 or 50-500 zoom extender 12.50
Angenieux 35-140mm zoom lens 25.00
Angenieux 35-350mm zoom lens 60.00
Silent zoom motor drive 12.50
Servo silent zoom motor drive 20.00
Computer zoom drive with 25-250 zoom lens 125.00

EXTRA BNC MAGAZINES
400' or 1000' 3.50
2000' 6.00

ADDITIONAL BNC MOTORS
Synchronous 110v AC or 220v AC 18.00
Crystal controlled 28v DC with BNC motor
       housing and 1-battery. Motor will also run at 12,
       16, 24, 25, and 32 F.P.S. 75.00
Extra batteries for crystal motor 15.00
Variable speed 12v DC or 110v AC-DC 12.00
Multi-duty 96v DC 25.00
Multi-duty control box 20.00

ACCESSORIES-REFLEX BNC CAMERAS
Worral gear head 15.00
Geared wedge 10.00
Obie light 3.50
Matte cutter 7.50
Periscope 10.00
Voltage regulator 110v 10.00

```
Voltage regulator 220v..............................  12.50
Reverter (transistorized) to use 220v motor
    from 110v source..............................  15.00
Reverter-regulator, compact combination of above .....  25.00
2-battery cases with siamese (less batteries) ..........  2.00
```

MITCHELL S35R MK II CAMERA
with 25, 50, 75mm lenses, follow focus, viewfinder,
2-1000' magazines, choice of variable speed or
sync motor 60.00

MITCHELL S35R MK II HIGH SPEED CAMERA
with 25, 50, 75mm lenses, follow focus, viewfinder,
2-1000' magazines, high speed and variable
speed motors 110.00

MITCHELL S35R MK II CAMERA AND BLIMP
with 25, 50, 75mm lenses, 2-1000' magazines, 110v
or 220v sync motor 95.00
as above but with zoom lens housing, 25-250 zoom
lens and zoom motor drive 150.00

ADDITIONAL S35R MK II LENSES
```
15mm to 150mm Kowa or Super Baltar        .......... 15.00
90mm Macro Kilar ...............................  7.50
203mm Cooke to 300mm........................... 15.00
400mm to 500mm with support .................... 20.00
600mm with support ............................ 25.00
800mm with support ............................ 30.00
1000mm-1200mm with support .................... 37.50
400-600-800-1200mm combi lens with support ........ 60.00
Angenieux 20-120mm zoom lens................... 80.00
Canon 25-120mm Macro zoom lens ................ 75.00
Angenieux 25-250mm zoom lens................... 55.00
40-400 or 50-500 zoom extender .................. 12.50
Angenieux 35-140mm zoom lens................... 25.00
Silent zoom motor drive......................... 12.50
Servo silent zoom motor drive.................... 20.00
Computer zoom drive with 25-250mm zoom lens ....... 125.00
```

EXTRA MARK II MAGAZINES
```
400' regular or inverted.........................  3.50
1000' ......................................  3.50
2000' ......................................  6.00
```

ADDITIONAL MARK II MOTORS
```
Variable speed 12v DC or 110v AC-DC............... 12.00
Synchronous 110v AC or 220v AC .................. 18.00
High speed motor — ordered with camera............ 40.00
                ordered without camera .......... 50.00
Stop motion motor — ordered with camera ........... 20.00
                ordered without camera ........ 30.00
Intervalometer or programmer.................... 12.50
```

ACCESSORIES MARK II CAMERAS
```
Mark II blimp.................................. 50.00
        with zoom extensions ..................... 60.00
Worral head................................... 15.00
Geared wedge          ......................... 10.00
Matte cutter ................................  7.50
Barney .....................................  6.00
Periscope.................................... 10.00
```

```
Pistol grip ........................................    2.50
Motor door. .......................................    7.50
Sync cable to Nagra ...............................    1.50
Voltage regulator 110v ............................   10.00
Voltage regulator 220v. ...........................   12.50
2-battery cases with siamese (less batteries) ........    2.00
```

F&B/CECO REFLEX MITCHELL NC CAMERA
with 40, 50, 75, 100mm lenses, viewfinder, 2-1000'
magazines, 110v or 220v sync motor 60.00

F&B/CECO REFLEX MITCHELL STANDARD CAMERA
with 40, 50, 75, 100mm lenses, viewfinder, 2-1000'
magazines 12v DC or 110v AC-DC
variable speed motor. 60.00

**HIGH SPEED F&B/CECO REFLEX MITCHELL
STANDARD CAMERA**
with 40, 50, 75, 100mm lenses, viewfinder, 2-1000'
magazines, high speed (128 F.P.S.) and
variable speed motor. 90.00

**ADDITIONAL LENSES FOR REFLEX NC AND
STANDARD CAMERAS**

```
28mm to 150mm. ..................................    5.00
90mm Macro Kilar ................................    7.50
300mm ...........................................   15.00
Angenieux 25-250mm zoom lens. ...................   55.00
40-400mm or 50-500mm zoom extender .............   12.50
Angenieux 35-140mm zoom lens. ...................   25.00
Silent zoom motor drive. ........................   12.50
```

EXTRA REFLEX NC OR STANDARD MAGAZINES

```
400' or 1000'. ...................................    3.50
2000'. ...........................................    6.00
```

ADDITIONAL MOTORS — REFLEX NC OR STANDARD

```
Synchronous 110v AC or 220v AC ..................   18.00
Crystal controlled 28v DC with 1-battery (NC only),
    motor will also run at 12, 16, 24, 25 or 32 FPS ....   75.00
Extra battery for crystal motor ..................   15.00
Variable speed 12v DC or 110v AC-DC. .............   12.00
High speed motor (Standard only) ................   40.00
Multi-Duty 96v DC ...............................   25.00
Multi-Duty control box ..........................   20.00
Stop motion motor — ordered with camera ..........   20.00
                    ordered without camera ........   30.00
Intervalometer ..................................   10.00
```

ACCESSORIES REFLEX NC OR STANDARD

```
Worral gear head ................................   15.00
Geared wedge. ...................................   10.00
Tilt or fixed wedge. .............................    5.00
Bridge plate. ...................................    1.50
Follow focus. ...................................   10.00
Matte cutter ....................................    7.50
Periscope. ......................................   10.00
Barney. .........................................    6.00
Voltage regulator 110v. ..........................   10.00
Voltage regulator 220v. ..........................   12.50
Reverter (transistorized) to use 220v motor
    from 110v source. ............................   15.00
```

Reverter-Regulator, compact combination of above 25.00
2-battery cases with siamese (less batteries) 2.00

ARRIFLEX 35 BL
Self blimped camera, crystal controlled motor,
speeds from 10 to 90 FPS, 32, 50, 75mm Cooke
lenses, 1-400' magazine, 1-battery .... Prices
400' 35 BL magazines .... to
1000' 35 BL magazines .... be
BL batteries .... announced

ARRIFLEX 35mm IICB CAMERA
with 32, 50, 75mm Cooke lenses, swing-away
matte box, 2-400' magazines, hi hat, variable
or constant speed motor and battery 35.00

ARRIFLEX 35mm IICB-GS CAMERA
with same equipment as above but with built in
sync generator and bloop light 40.00

ARRIFLEX 35mm HIGH SPEED IICB CAMERA
with 32, 50, 75mm Cooke lenses, swing-away matte
box, 2-400' magazines, hi hat, variable and high
speed motors, 2-batteries 60.00

ARRIFLEX 35mm IICB TECHNISCOPE CAMERA
with 32, 50, 75mm Cooke lenses, swing-away matte
box, 2-400' magazines hi hat, variable or constant
speed motor, 1-battery 55.00

ARRIFLEX 35mm IICB CAMERA WITH BLIMP
with 32, 50, 75mm Cooke lenses, 400' blimp,
2-400' magazines, 110v sync motor 65.00

ARRIFLEX 35mm IICB CAMERA WITH 120S BLIMP
with 32, 50, 75mm Cooke lenses, 120S blimp, and
zoom extensions, 2-400' magazines, 110v sync motor ... 80.00
above including 25-250 zoom lens 135.00

ARRIFLEX 35mm IICB CAMERA WITH PLASTIC BLIMP
with 32, 50, 75mm Cooke lenses, Cine 60 plastic
blimp, 2-400' magazines, constant speed motor,
offset motor base, 1-battery 70.00
Zoom door for plastic blimp 5.00

ADDITIONAL LENSES ARRIFLEX 35mm CAMERAS
9.8mm Tegea with sunshade 12.50
16mm Zeiss Distagon 12.50
14.5mm — 100mm 7.50
125mm — 300mm 15.00
400mm — 500mm with support 20.00
600mm with support 25.00
800mm with support 30.00
1000mm to 1200mm with support 37.50
1500mm Questar with sports finder 50.00
400-600-800-1200mm Combi lens with support 60.00
Kinoptik 1:1 ratio lenses, 50mm, 75mm, or 100mm 12.50
Bellows extension with 91mm lens 7.50
Lens extention tube 1.25

```
Fisheye lens adapter .............................    10.00
Angenieux 30-120mm zoom lens ...................    00.00
Canon 25-120mm Macro zoom lens ...............    75.00
Angenieux 25-250mm zoom lens...................    55.00
40-400 or 50-500 zoom extender .................    12.50
Silent zoom motor drive..........................    12.50
Angenieux 35-140mm zoom lens..................    25.00
```

MAGASINES-ARRIFLEX 35mm CAMERAS

Daily

```
200' .........................................     3.00
400' .........................................     4.00
1000' ........................................     6.00
```

MOTORS-ARRIFLEX 35mm CAMERAS

```
16v DC constant speed or variable speed ............     7.50
16v DC crystal controlled (24 F.P.S.) ................    50.00
32v DC high speed with rheostat ..................    30.00
110v AC/DC variable speed .......................     7.50
110v AC synchronous............................    12.50
Offset motor base..............................    10.00
```

ACCESSORIES-ARRIFLEX 35mm CAMERAS

```
Battery — 16v belt or pack ......................     5.00
Periscopic finder...............................     7.50
Sync generator ................................     7.00
Sync cable ...................................     1.50
Siamese battery cable .........................     1.00
Blimp 400'....................................    20.00
Blimp 120S with zoom extension ..................    40.00
Blimp — Cine 60 plastic .........................    25.00
Zoom door for plastic blimp ......................     5.00
Sound Barney.................................     5.00
Heater Barney.................................     7.50
Underwater housing............................    75.00
Shoulder pod..................................     1.50
Hi hat tripod adapter ..........................     1.00
```

F&B/CECO REFLEX EYEMO 35mm CAMERA
with 28, 50, 75mm Angenieux lenses................   40.00

F&B/CECO REFLEX EYEMO 35mm CAMERA
with 50mm Super Balter lens......................   50.00

ADDITIONAL LENSES REFLEX EYEMO 35mm CAMERAS

```
Angenieux or Baltar 28mm to 150mm ...............     5.00
Super Baltar 20, 25, 35, 75, 100, 150mm...........    15.00
Zoom lens 36-82mm...........................    20.00
```

ACCESSORIES-REFLEX EYEMO CAMERAS

```
200' or 400' magazine ..........................     2.50
12v or 24v DC variable speed motor................     7.50
110v AC-DC variable speed motor ..................     7.50
110v AC synchronous motor ......................     7.50
```

35MM CAMERAS

Daily

MITCHELL BNC CAMERA
with 25, 32, 40, 50, 75, 100mm Cooke lenses, 4-1000
magazines, viewfinder, 110v or 220v sync motor 100.00

MITCHELL BNC TECHNISCOPE CAMERA
with 25, 32, 40, 50, 75, 100mm Cooke lenses, 4-1000'
magazines, viewfinder, 110v or 220v sync motor 135.00

MITCHELL BNC SCANASCOPE CAMERA
with 50, 75, 100mm anamorphic lenses, 4-1000'
magazines, viewfinder, 110v or 220v sync motor 150.00

ADDITIONAL BNC LENSES
14.5 or 18mm	15.00
25mm to 150mm.	12.50
50mm f.0.95 ultra fast lens	40.00
Berthiot 38-154mm zoom lens with finder	35.00
Berthiot 60-240mm zoom lens with finder	35.00
Angenieux 24-240mm zoom lens with finder	85.00
Lens extension tubes	3.50
Bellows extension with 91mm lens	12.50
Selsyn follow focus	15.00
Variable diffuser	12.50
Variable anamorphic	30.00
6 image revolving prism	12.50

EXTRA MAGAZINES — BNC CAMERAS
400'	3.50
1000'	3.50
2000'	6.00

MOTORS — BNC CAMERAS
Synchronous 110v AC or 220v AC	18.00
Crystal controlled 28v DC with BNC motor housing and 1-battery. Motor will also run at 12, 16, 24, 25, and 32 F.P.S.	75.00
Extra battery for crystal motor	15.00
Variable speed 12v DC or 110v AC-DC.	12.00
Multi-Duty 96v DC	25.00
Multi-Duty control box	20.00

ACCESSORIES — BNC CAMERAS
Worral gear head	15.00
Geared wedge	10.00
Obie light	3.50
Matte cutter	7.50
Periscope.	10.00
Voltage regulator 110v.	10.00
Voltage regulator 220v.	12.50
Reverter (transistorized) to use 220 motor from 110v source.	15.00
Reverter-Regulator, compact combination of above	25.00
2-battery cases with siamese (less batteries)	2.00

MITCHELL NC CAMERA
with 40, 50, 75, 100mm Cooke lenses, viewfinder,
2-1000' magazines, 110v or 220v sync motor 35.00

MITCHELL NC SCANASCOPE CAMERA
with 40, 50, 75, 100mm anamorphic lenses,
viewfinder, follow focus, 2-1000' magazines, 110v or
220v sync motor. 125.00

MITCHELL STANDARD CAMERA
with 40, 50, 75, 100mm lenses, viewfinder, 2-1000'
magazines, 12v DC or 110v AC-DC variable speed
motor 30.00

```
┌────────────────────────────────────────────────────────────────┐
│ HIGH SPEED MITCHELL STANDARD CAMERA                             │
│   with 40, 50, 75, 100mm lenses, viewfinder, 2-1000             │
│   magazines, high speed (128 F.P.S.) and variable              │
│   speed motors . . . . . . . . . . . . . . . . . . . . .  75.00 │
└────────────────────────────────────────────────────────────────┘
```

ADDITIONAL LENSES — NC OR STANDARD CAMERAS

14.5 or 18mm	7.50
25mm to 100mm	5.00
125mm to 205mm	7.50
250mm to 500mm	12.50
Berthiot 38-154mm zoom lens with finder	35.00
Berthiot 60-240mm zoom lens with finder	35.00
Lens extension tubes	3.50
Bellows focusing extension with 91mm lens	7.50
Follow focus device	10.00
Variable diffuser	7.50
Variable anamorphic	30.00
6 image revolving prism	12.50

EXTRA MAGAZINES-NC OR STANDARD CAMERAS

400'	3.50
1000'	3.50
2000'	6.00

MOTORS-NC OR STANDARD CAMERAS

Synchronous 110v AC or 220v AC	18.00
Crystal controlled 28v DC with 1-battery (NC only) motor will also run at 12, 16, 24, 25 and 32 FPS	75.00
Extra battery for crystal motor	15.00
Variable speed 12v DC or 110v AC-DC	12.00
High speed motor (Standard only)	40.00
Multi-Duty 96v DC	25.00
Multi-Duty control box	20.00
Stop motion motor — ordered with camera	20.00
ordered without camera	30.00
Intervalometer	10.00

ACCESSORIES-NC OR STANDARD CAMERAS

Worral gear head	15.00
Bridge plate for gear head	1.50
Geared wedge	10.00
Tilt wedge	5.00
Matte cutter	7.50
Periscope	10.00
Barney	6.00
Voltage regulator 110v	10.00
Voltage regulator 220v	12.50
Reverter (transistorized) to use 220v motors from 110v source	15.00
Reverter-Regulator, compact combination of above	25.00
2-battery cases with siamese (less batteries)	2.00

```
┌────────────────────────────────────────────────────────────────┐
│ BELL & HOWELL EYEMO 35mm CAMERA                                 │
│   with 35, 50, 75mm lenses . . . . . . . . . . . . .  15.00     │
└────────────────────────────────────────────────────────────────┘
```

ADDITIONAL LENSES-EYEMO CAMERAS

18.5mm	7.50
25mm to 100mm	5.00
125mm to 9"	7.50
10" and over	10.00

ACCESSORIES-EYEMO CAMERAS

200' or 400' magazine	2.50

```
Shiftover block ...................................   3.00
12v or 24v DC variable speed motor..................   7.50
110v AC-DC variable speed motor ....................   7.50
110v AC synchronous motor ..........................   7.50
```

SEE "STILL CAMERAS" FOR FILM STRIP AND SINGLE
ADVANCE EYEMOS

ANAMORPHIC LENSES

TODD-AO 35-anamorphic lenses for BNC,
BNC-Reflex, S35R MkII and Arriflex Cameras: Weekly
28mm (Arriflex only)................................150.00
38mm, 50mm, 75mm, 100mm, 200mm
      macro telephoto............................150.00
50-500mm motorized zoom lens 300.00

ACCESSORIES-TODD-AO 35
```
Wide angle matte box................................  15.00
Arri matte box bracket..............................   5.00
S35R matte box bracket..............................   5.00
S35R follow focus with cam and finder ..............  50.00
Filters, diffusions, fogs, graduates.......... each   3.00
```

                            Daily

SCANASCOPE LENSES FOR BNC
50mm, 75mm or 100mm with matte box 25.00

SCANASCOPE LENSES FOR NC
40mm, 50mm, 75mm, or 100mm with matte box 25.00

SCANASCOPE OR ULTRASCOPE LENSES FOR ARRIFLEX
40mm, 50mm, 75mm, 85mm, 100mm or 400mm with
matte box... 25.00

Canon 50-240mm zoom .... rates to be announced

16MM CAMERAS   Daily

```
ARRIFLEX BL 16mm CAMERA
   with self blimped 9.5-95mm zoom lens, matte box,
   110v synchronous or 12v DC constant speed motor
   with 1-battery, 1-400' magazine...................  80.00
```

```
ARRIFLEX BL 16mm CAMERA
   with self blimped 12-120mm zoom lens, matte box,
   110v synchronous or 12v DC constant speed motor
   with 1-battery, 1-400' magazine...................  75.00
```

```
ARRIFLEX BL 16mm CAMERA
   with self blimped 12-120mm zoom lens and silent
   zoom motor, with built in hand control, matte box,
   110v synchronous or 12v DC constant speed motor
   with 1-battery, 1-400' magazine...................  90.00
```

```
ARRIFLEX BL 16mm CRYSTAL CONTROLLED CAMERA
   with self blimped 12-120mm zoom lens, matte box,
   universal motor with precision crystal motor
   control, 1-400' magazine..........................125.00
   if with 9.5-95mm zoom lens .......................130.00
```

ARRIFLEX BL 16mm CAMERA WITH SINGLE SYSTEM MAGNETIC SOUND

With self blimped 12-120mm zoom lens, matte box,
110v synchronous or 12v DC constant speed motor
and battery, 1-400' magazine, single system module,
amplifier and mike.................................110.00
if with 9.5-95mm zoom lens 115.00

ACCESSORIES-ARRIFLEX BL 16mm CAMERA

400' magazine....................................	7.50
1200' magazine...................................	12.50
400' magazine barney	3.50
12 volt hip or belt battery........................	6.00
110v AC synchronous motor.......................	12.50
12v DC constant speed motor.....................	7.50
Precision crystal motor control with 1-battery..........	50.00
Extra battery for precision crystal motor control........	10.00
Single system magnetic module with amplifier	
ordered with camera......................	35.00
ordered without camera	45.00
Universal lens housing............................	12.50
Offset eyepiece..................................	7.50
Periscopic finder.................................	7.50
BL body brace...................................	3.50
BL variable speed control	10.00

ARRIFLEX S/B 16mm CAMERA

with 17.5, 25, 50mm Cooke lenses, matte box,
variable or constant speed motor, 1-8v battery 30.00

ARRIFLEX S/B 16mm CAMERA WITH BLIMP

with 17.5, 25, 50mm Cooke lenses, 110v AC sync
motor, 2-400' magazines, 1-torque motor 65.00

ADDITIONAL LENSES-ARRIFLEX S/B 16mm CAMERA

5.7 Tegea, 5.9 Angenieux or 8mm Distagon	10.00
9mm to 100mm..................................	7.50
125mm to 300mm	15.00
400mm to 500mm with support	20.00
600mm with support	25.00
800mm with support	30.00
1000mm to 1200mm with support	37.50
1500mm Questar with sports finder................	50.00
400-600-800-1200mm Combi lens with support.......	60.00
Kinoptik 1:1 ratio lenses, 50mm, 75mm or 100mm......	12.50
Bellows extension with 91mm lens	7.50
Lens extension	1.25
Fisheye lens adapter	10.00
Angenieux 9.5 to 95mm zoom lens	35.00
Angenieux 12 to 120mm zoom lens.................	30.00
Zoom motor for above	10.00
Canon 12 to 120mm Macro zoom lens	30.00
Angenieux 12 to 240mm 20:1 zoom lens	55.00
Angenieux 15 to 150mm zoom lens.................	30.00
Berthiot 17 to 70mm, 17 to 85mm or 25 to 100mm	
zoom lenses	12.50
Angenieux 25 to 250mm zoom lens.................	55.00
40-400mm or 50-500mm zoom extender..............	12.50
Silent zoom motor drive for 25-250	12.50

ADDITIONAL MOTORS-ARRIFLEX S/B 16mm CAMERA

8v variable speed 7.50

```
8v constant speed...............................  7.50
110v AC synchronous............................ 12.50
2-speed stop motion (AC only)..................... 20.00
Intervalometer ................................. 10.00
```

ACCESSORIES-ARRIFLEX S/B 16mm CAMERA
```
400' magazine....................................  3.50
Magazine torque take up motor....................  4.00
Sync pulse generator installed ..................  6.00
Sync cable......................................  1.50
8v battery (belt or pack)........................  4.00
8/16v battery (belt or pack).....................  5.00
Periscope finder................................  7.50
Sports finder...................................  3.50
Arri 400' blimp (less motor).................... 20.00
Blimp zoom extension for 12 to 120 .............  7.50
Underwater housing 100' w/o camera ............. 50.00
Underwater housing 400' w/o camera ............. 75.00
Barney..........................................  5.00
Heater Barney...................................  7.50
Pistol grip ....................................  1.00
Shoulder pod....................................  1.50
Shoulder brace .................................  3.50
```

ECLAIR NPR 16mm CAMERA
with 15, 25, 50mm "C" mount lenses, matte box,
12v DC constant speed motor with sync and bloop
and 1-battery or 110v AC sync motor, 1-400'
magazine 55.00

ECLAIR NPR 16mm CAMERA
with 15, 25, 50mm "C" mount lenses, matte box,
12v Beala crystal motor (may also be used as
variable speed motor) 1-battery, 1-400' magazine..... 90.00

ECLAIR NPR SUPER 16mm CAMERA
Enlarged aperature for blow up to 35mm. Lens
mount moved to new optical center and special
ground glass installed. Camera with 12v DC
constant speed motor with sync and bloop and
1-battery or 110v AC sync motor, 1-400' magazine ... 75.00
if with Beala crystal motor........................110.00

ECLAIR ACL 16mm CAMERA
with 15, 25, 50mm "C" mount lenses, gel filter
holder, crystal 24 FPS motor, battery with 1/2
hour recharger, 2-200' magazines, pistol grip......... 60.00

ADDITIONAL LENSES-ECLAIR NPR OR ACL 16mm CAMERAS
```
5.7 Tegea, 5.9 Angenieux or 8mm Distagon ........... 10.00
9mm to 100mm Arri mount ........................  7.50
10mm to 152mm "C" mount ........................  5.00
125mm to 300mm Arri mount ...................... 15.00
For additional Telephoto Lenses See Arriflex S/B
40mm or 90mm Macro Kilar .......................  7.50
Kinoptik 1:1 ratio lenses, 50mm, 75mm, 100mm ....... 12.50
Fisheye lens adapter ........................... 10.00
Angenieux 9.5 to 95mm zoom lens ................ 35.00
Angenieux 12 to 120mm zoom lens................. 30.00
Zoom motor drive for above..................... 10.00
Canon 12 to 120mm Macro zoom lens .............. 30.00
Angenieux 12 to 240mm 20:1 zoom lens ........... 55.00
```

```
Angenieux 15 to 150mm zoom lens..................   30.00
Berthiot 17 to 70mm, 17 to 85mm or 25 to 100mm
        zoom lens........................   12.50
Angenieux 25 to 250mm zoom lens..................   55.00
40-400mm or 50-500mm extender...................   12.50
Silent zoom motor drive for 25 to 250...............   12.50
```

ADDITIONAL MOTORS-ECLAIR NPR CAMERA
```
Constant speed 12v DC..........................   12.50
Variable speed 12v DC...........................   12.50
Synchronous 110v AC ...........................   12.50
Beala crystal sync (may be used as variable speed) .....   40.00
```

ADDITIONAL ACCESSORIES-ECLAIR NPR AND ACL CAMERAS
```
400' NPR magazine ............................   15.00
200' ACL magazine .............................   15.00
400' ACL magazine....................... to be announced
NPR 12v battery (hip or belt) .....................   6.00
NPR Frezzo magazine contour battery...............   6.00
ACL battery.................................   5.00
ACL battery charger...........................   5.00
Sync cable.................................   1.50
Barney....................................   5.00
IMEREC upright finder for NPR ...................   7.50
F&B/Ceco brace for NPR.........................   2.50
Leopod brace for NPR ..........................   5.00
```

F&B/CECO AURICON CINEVOICE CONVERSION 16mm SOUND CAMERA
with 15, 25, 50mm lenses, finder door, 110v AC
sync motor, 2-400' magazines:
```
    silent...............................   35.00
    with optical sound.......................   40.00
    with magnetic sound......................   50.00
```

F&B/CECO AURICON CINEVOICE CONVERSION 16mm SOUND CAMERA with TVT SHUTTER
with 15, 25, 50mm lenses, finder door, 110v AC
sync motor, 2-400' magazines:
```
    silent...............................   40.00
    with optical sound.......................   45.00
    with magnetic sound......................   55.00
```

F&B/CECO AURICON CINEVOICE CONVERSION 16mm SOUND CAMERA with CINESYNC
Crystal controlled 12v AC motor for double or
single system sound. With 15, 25, 50mm lenses,
2-400' magazines and 12v Cinesync battery:
```
    silent...............................   70.00
    with optical sound.......................   75.00
    with magnetic sound......................   85.00
```
Cinesync camera as above, but with 12 to 120mm
zoom lens, short finder, heavy duty lens mount
and zoom door .... add   35.00

F&B/CECO AURICON CINEVOICE CONVERSION 16mm SOUND CAMERA with CORDLESS CRYSTAL SYNC
Built in crystal controlled inverter with replaceable
nickle cadmium battery, can also run off 110v AC.
Double system or single system magnetic sound.
2-400' magazines, 12 to 120mm Angenieux zoom lens:
```
    silent...............................   120.00
    with magnetic sound......................   135.00
```

SUPER 16 F&B/CECO AURICON CONVERSION with CORDLESS CRYSTAL SYNC

Enlarged aperature for blow up to 35mm. Lens mount moved to new optical center. Special 12 to 120mm Angenieux zoom lens with short finder and super 16 reticle. Camera has built in crystal controlled inverter with replaceable nickel cadmium battery, can also run off 110v AC. 2-400' magazines ... 140.00

AURICON PRO 600 16mm SOUND CAMERA

with 15, 25, 50mm lenses, 110v AC sync motor
2-600' magazines:

silent.	35.00
with optical sound	40.00
with magnetic sound	50.00

AURICON SUPER 1200 16mm SOUND CAMERA

with 15, 25, 50mm lenses, 110v AC sync motor, 2-1200' magazines:

silent.	50.00
with optical sound	60.00
with magnetic sound..,	70.00

ADDITIONAL LENSES-AURICON CAMERAS

5.7 Tegea, 5.9 Angenieux or 16mm Distagon	10.00
10mm to 152mm "C" mount	5.00
FOR ADDITIONAL TELEPHOTO LENSES SEE ARRIFLEX S/B	
Angenieux 9.5 to 95mm zoom lens w/finder.	40.00
Angenieux 12 to 120mm zoom lens w/finder	35.00
Angenieux 12 to 240mm 20:1 zoom lens w/finder.	60.00
Angenieux 15 to 150mm zoom lens w/finder	35.00
Zoom motor drive for above lenses	10.00
Berthiot 17 to 70 or 17 to 85mm zoom lens w/finder	15.00

ADDITIONAL MAGAZINES-AURICON CAMERAS

400' Mitchell or Auricon	3.50
600' Auricon	5.00
1200' Mitchell or Auricon	6.00

POWER SUPPLIES 110v AC-AURICON CAMERAS

Frezzolini 100D.	20.00
100DC (crystal).	40.00
1000DX with 1-battery	25.00
1000DXC (crystal) with 1-battery	50.00
Extra 1000DX or DXC battery	7.50
External 1000DX or DXC battery charger	5.00
Extra battery for Cine sync camera	6.00
Extra battery for cordless camera	7.50

BEAULIEU RBT 16mm CAMERA

with 15, 25, 50mm lenses, semi-automatic exposure meter, built in electric motor, pistol grip, battery and charger. ... 20.00

ADDITIONAL LENSES-BEAULIEU CAMERA

5.7 Tegea, 5.9 Angenieux or 8mm Distagon	10.00
10mm to 152mm "C" mount	5.00
200mm to 300mm	15.00
40mm or 90mm Macro	7.50
Kinoptik 1:1 ratio lenses, 50mm, 75mm or 100mm	12.50

Fisheye lens adapter 10.00
Angenieux 9.5 to 95mm zoom lens 35.00
Angenieux 12 to 120mm zoom lens 30.00
Canon 12 to 120mm Macro zoom lens 30.00
Angenieux 12 to 240mm zoom lens 55.00
Angenieux 15 to 150mm zoom lens 30.00
Berthiot 17 to 70mm or 17 to 85mm zoom lens 12.00

ACCESSORIES-BEAULIEU 16mm CAMERA
200' magazine with built in torque motor 3.00
Pocket battery and charger 1.50
Extra battery for pistol grip 1.50
Base plate 1.25
AC power converter 2.50
Sync generator 3.50
Sync cable 1.50

BELL & HOWELL FILMO HIGH SPEED 16mm CAMERA
with 15, 25, 50mm lenses, sports finder, speed to
128 FPS 25.00

BELL & HOWELL FILMO 16mm CAMERA
with 15, 25, 50mm lenses, gel filter holder 15.00

ADDITIONAL LENSES-B & H FILMO CAMERAS
5.7 Tegea, 5.9 Angenieux or 8mm Distagon 10.00
10mm to 152mm "C" mount 5.00
200mm to 300mm 15.00
Angenieux 9.5 to 95mm zoom lens with finder 40.00
Angenieux 12 to 120mm zoom lens with finder 35.00
Angenieux 12 to 240mm zoom lens with finder 60.00
Angenieux 15 to 150mm zoom lens with finder 35.00
Berthiot 17 to 70mm or 17 to 85mm zoom lens
       with finder 15.00
Zoom motor drive 10.00

ACCESSORIES — B & H FILMO
200' magazine 1.50
400' magazine 3.00
Variable speed motor 12v DC or 110v AC-DC 5.00
Synchronous motor 110v AC 7.50
High speed motor (128 FPS) 110v AC-DC 15.00
Focusing prism 1.50

BOLEX REX 16mm CAMERA
with 15, 25, 50mm lenses 20.00

BOLEX REX 5 16mm CAMERA
with 15, 25, 50mm lenses, 400' magazine and torque
motor, MST constant speed camera motor with built
in sync generator, battery and charger 40.00

ADDITIONAL LENSES-BOLEX CAMERAS
5.7mm Tegea, 5.9mm Angenieux or 8mm Distagon 10.00
10mm to 152mm "C" mount 5.00
FOR ADDITIONAL TELEPHOTO LENSES
     SEE ARRIFLEX S/B
40mm or 90mm Macro 7.50
Kinoptik 1:1 ratio lenses, 50mm, 75mm, 100mm 12.50
Angenieux 9.5 to 95mm zoom lens 35.00
Angenieux 12 to 120mm zoom lens 30.00
Canon 12 to 120mm Macro zoom lens 30.00
Angenieux 12 to 240mm 20:1 zoom lens 55.00

```
Angenieux 15 to 150mm zoom lens..................    30.00
Berthiot 17 to 70mm or 17 to 85mm zoom lens.........    12.50
Zoom motor drive................................    10.00
Lens extension tube.............................     1.25
Fisheye lens adapter............................    10.00
```

ACCESSORIES-BOLEX CAMERAS
```
MST constant speed motor......................     7.50
Battery for MST motor..........................     5.00
Sync cable.....................................     1.50
110v AC synchronous motor......................     7.50
400' magazine for Rex 5........................     5.00
Take up motor for magazine.....................     2.50
Rex-o-fader....................................     1.50
Matte box......................................     2.50
Pistol grip....................................     1.50
```

DOIFLEX 16 REFLEX 16mm CAMERA
with 12.5, 25, 50mm Kino Cosmicar lenses,
8v variable speed motor, matte box, battery,
pistol grip......................................   20.00

DOIFLEX 16 REFLEX 16mm CAMERA
with Angenieux 12 to 120mm zoom lens, zoom
support bracket, 8v variable speed motor,
matte box, battery, pistol grip....................   50.00

ADDITIONAL LENSES-DOIFLEX CAMERA
```
5.7mm Tegea, 5.9mm Angenieux or 8mm Distagon......    10.00
10mm to 152mm "C" mount........................     5.00
    FOR ADDITIONAL TELEPHOTO LENSES
        SEE ARRIFLEX S/B
40mm or 90mm Macro.............................     7.50
Kinoptik 1:1 ratio lenses, 50mm, 75mm, 100mm.......    12.50
Fisheye lens adapter...........................    10.00
Angenieux 9.5 to 95mm zoom lens................    35.00
Angenieux 12 to 120mm zoom lens................    30.00
Canon 12 to 120mm Macro zoom lens..............    30.00
Angenieux 12 to 240mm zoom lens................    55.00
Angenieux 15 to 150mm zoom lens................    30.00
Berthiot 17 to 70mm or 17 to 85mm zoom lens.........    12.50
Zoom motor drive...............................    10.00
Lens extension tube............................     1.25
```

ACCESSORIES-DOIFLEX CAMERA
```
110v AC Stop motion motor......................    10.00
Intervalometer.................................    10.00
Extra variable speed motor.....................     5.00
Extra battery..................................     4.00
```

GSAP HELMET 16mm CAMERA
GSAP Camera with 15mm or 25mm lens mounted
in sky diver helmet. 1-battery....................   25.00
2-GSAP Cameras mounted in helmet...............   40.00

KODAK CINE SPECIAL 16mm CAMERA
with 15, 25, 50mm or 63mm lenses:
    with 100' magazine.........................   15.00
    with 200' magazine.........................   20.00

ADDITIONAL LENSES-CINE SPECIAL
```
5.7mm Tegea, 5.9mm Angenieux or 8mm Distagon......    10.00
10mm to 152mm "S" or "C" mount.................     5.00
```

FOR ADDITIONAL TELEPHOTO LENSES
    SEE ARRIFLEX S/B
40mm or 90mm Macro 7.50
Microflite 1:1 ratio lenses, 60mm 75mm 100mm 12.50
Angenieux 9.5 to 95mm zoom lens with finder 40.00
Angenieux 12 to 120mm zoom lens with finder 35.00
Angenieux 12 to 240mm zoom lens with finder 60.00
Angenieux 15 to 150mm zoom lens with finder 35.00
Berthiot 17 to 70mm or 17 to 85mm zoom lens
        with finder 15.00
Zoom motor drive 10.00

ACCESSORIES CINE SPECIAL
100' magazine 3.00
200' magazine 6.00
Synchronous motor 110v AC 7.50
Variable speed motor 12v DC or 110v AC-DC 7.50
Stop motion motor 110v AC 20.00
Intervalometer 10.00
F&B/CECO blimp 15.00
F&B/CECO blimp with finder, and 110v sync motor 20.00
Automatic dissolve control 2.50

KODAK K-100 16mm CAMERA
    with 15, 25, 63mm lenses 15.00
    10mm to 152mm lenses 5.00
    Underwater housing 25.00
    for zoom lenses see Kodak Cine Special

CANON SCOOPIC 16mm CAMERA
    with built in 13 to 76mm zoom lens, automatic
    exposure control, 2-rechargeable batteries
    with charger 25.00
        additional batteries 1.50
        additional charger 1.75
        Underwater housing 30.00

MITCHELL 16mm CAMERA
    with 17.5, 20, 25 and 35mm lenses, matte box,
    viewfinder, 3-400' magazines, 110v AC-DC variable
    speed or 110v or 220v AC sync motor 35.00

MITCHELL 16mm HIGH SPEED CAMERA
    with 17.5, 20, 25 and 35mm lenses, matte box,
    viewfinder, 3-400' magazines, 110v AC-DC
    high speed (128 FPS) motor 75.00

ADDITIONAL LENSES-MITCHELL 16mm CAMERA
5.7 Tegea, 5.9 Angenieux or 8mm Distagon 10.00
9mm to 152mm 5.00
90mm Macro 7.50
200mm to 300mm 15.00
400mm to 500mm with support 20.00
600mm with support 25.00
800mm with support 30.00
1000-1200mm with support 37.50
400-600-800-1200mm Combi lens 60.00
Angenieux 9.5 to 95mm zoom lens with finder 40.00
Angenieux 12 to 120mm zoom lens with finder 35.00
Angenieux 12 to 240mm zoom lens with finder 60.00

Angenieux 15 to 150mm zoom lens with finder 35.00
Berthiot 17 to 70mm or 17 to 85mm zoom lens
    with finder 15.00
Lens extension tube 3.50
Bellows lens extension with 91mm lens 7.50

ACCESSORIES-MITCHELL 16mm CAMERA
400' magazine. 3.50
1200' magazine. 6.00
Follow focus. 10.00
400' blimp 20.00
1200' blimp 25.00
High speed camera door 15.00
Variable speed motor 12v DC or 110v AC-DC 10.00
Synchronous 110v or 220v 12.50
Stop motion 110v AC (3 speed). 20.00
Intervalometer 10.00

16MM HIGH SPEED CAMERAS
Daily

NOVA 16-1
100' capacity, choice of one lens from 13mm to
150mm, power supply, double timing lights,
boresight, speed range from 200 to 8,500 FPS 50.00

NOVA 16-3
400' capacity choice of one lens from 13mm to
150mm, power supply, double timing lights,
boresight, magazine, speed range from 200 to
10,000 FPS. 60.00

FASTAX WF-4
400' capacity, with 50mm lens (accepts all "C"
mount lenses) 150v variac, speed range from
350 to 9000 FPS 60.00

EASTMAN (MAGNIFAX)
100' capacity, 63mm lens, built in speed selector,
timing light, oscilloscope recording device
installed, speed range from 1000 to 3000 FPS 50.00

LOCAM
Registration pin, intermittent movement, 100',
200' or 400' capacity on daylight spools, accepts
all "C" mount lenses, with 50mm lens, boresight
DC motor with 30v battery or 110v AC motor 90.00

ACCESSORIES-LOCAM CAMERA
Extra Locam battery. 10.00
Angenieux 9.5 to 95mm zoom lens with finder. 40.00
Angenieux 12 to 120mm zoom lens with finder 35.00
Angenieux 12 to 240mm zoom lens with finder 60.00
5.7 Tegea, 5.9 Angenieux or 8mm Distagon lens 10.00
10mm to 152mm "C" mount lenses. 5.00
FOR ADDITIONAL TELEPHOTO LENSES
    SEE ARRIFLEX S/B
High speed exposure meter. 10.00

ACCESSORIES-NOVA CAMERAS

```
400' magazine (daylight spool) . . . . . . . . . . . . . . . . . . . . . .   10.00
Extra 400' balanced spool . . . . . . . . . . . . . . . . . . . . . . . .    3.00
Camera and events synchronizer . . . . . . . . . . . . . . . . . .    7.50
Electronic flash amplifier . . . . . . . . . . . . . . . . . . . . . . . . .   7.50
Timing light generator . . . . . . . . . . . . . . . . . . . . . . . . . . .   7.50
Portable, rechargeable power supply . . . . . . . . . . . . . . . .  15.00
High speed exposure meter . . . . . . . . . . . . . . . . . . . . . . .  10.00
```

FILM STRIP, 70MM AND STILL CAMERAS   Daily

EYEMO 35mm FILMSTRIP CAMERA
with 90mm Macro Kilar lens and 54mm wide
angle adapter, reflex viewing, single frame
advance, filmstrip aperature 30.00

EYEMO 35mm SINGLE LENS CAMERA
single frame advance, film strip aperature, choice of
one lens from 25mm to 100mm 15.00

HULCHER MODEL 102 70mm CAMERA
100' capacity, 101mm or 162mm lenses 110v AC
to DC rectifier, remote cable, speeds from 5 to
20 FPS or single frame 50.00

```
Sync strobe for Hulcher with slave head and
         power supply . . . . . . . . . . . . . . . . . . . . . . . . . . . . .  15.00
Speed Graphic with lens, flashgun and holders . . . . . . . .   7.50
8 x 10 Viewcamera with 12" lens and holders . . . . . . . . .  10.00
Polaroid Camera with wink light . . . . . . . . . . . . . . . . . . . .   5.00
Nikonos underwater Nikon with 35mm lens . . . . . . . . . .  10.00
Underwater exposure meter . . . . . . . . . . . . . . . . . . . . . .  10.00
```

UNDERWATER CAMERAS

35mm ARRIFLEX IICB CAMERA
with underwater housing, 18mm lens, 2-400'
magazines, constant speed motor, battery 110.00

35mm Arriflex underwater housing only 75.00

35mm EYEMO REFLEX CAMERA
with underwater housing, 100' capacity, spring
wound, with wide angle lens 75.00

35mm Eyemo reflex underwater housing only 35.00

16mm ARRIFLEX S/B CAMERA (100')
with underwater housing, (100' capacity), 11.5mm
lens, constant speed motor, battery 80.00

16mm Arriflex 100' underwater housing only 50.00

16mm ARRIFLEX S/B CAMERA (400')
with underwater housing, 11.5mm lens, 2-400'
magazines, torque motor, constant speed motor,
battery 110.00

16mm Arriflex 400′ underwater housing only 75.00

16mm REBIKOFF CINEMARINE
UNDERWATER CAMERA
  Integral battery operated, variable speed motor,
  distortion free compensating lens; can be
  pressurized to depths of 800 ft., weightless in
  water. With 10mm f 1.8 lens, 200′ film capacity 100.00

16mm KODAK K-100 CAMERA
  with underwater housing, 10mm lens, 100′ capacity,
  spring wound 40′ run per wind 40.00

K-100 underwater housing only 25.00
Underwater exposure meter 10.00

TRIPOD HEADS AND LEGS
Daily

F&B/Ceco Pro Jr fluid head (ball level) with legs.	7.50
F&B/Ceco Pro Jr friction head with legs.	5.00
F&B/Ceco Pro Jr geared or spring head with legs	5.00
F&B/Ceco Pro Jr standard or baby legs only	2.50
F&B/Ceco Pro Jr hi hat on board.	1.00
F&B/Ceco Pro Jr wedge.	3.50
F&B/Ceco Pro Jr airplane bracket: small	5.00
large	7.50
F&B/Ceco Balanced tripod head	7.50
F&B/Ceco gyro head with legs	10.00
F&B/Ceco gyro baby legs	2.50
F&B/Ceco gyro hi hat on board	2.50
Akeley gyro head with legs	10.00
Akeley standard or baby legs	3.50
Akeley hi hat on board	3.00
Arriflex ball friction head with legs	5.00
Arriflex ball standard or baby legs.	3.50
Arriflex ball hi hat on board	3.00
Gimbal tripod legs with weights	15.00
Miller "DF" fluid head with Pro Jr legs	5.00
Miller "Pro" fluid head with Pro Jr legs.	7.50
Mitchell friction or geared head.	7.50
Mitchell legs all sizes	3.50
Mitchell hi hat on board	3.00
Metal tripod legs	5.00
Moy geared head.	15.00
Moy wedge.	2.50
NCE fluid head with legs	7.50
NCE standard or baby legs	3.50
NCE hi hat on board	3.00
O'Connor 100 fluid head only	12.50
O'Connor 100 ball level	2.50
O'Connor 50 fluid head only.	10.00
Pro Jr legs for O'Connor 50	2.50
Pro Jr ball level for O'Connor 50	2.50
Sachtler-Wolf double gyro head and legs	15.00
Sachtler-Wolf standard or baby legs.	3.50
Sachtler-Wolf hi hat on board	3.00
Worral gear head	15.00
Small wheel for Worral head	3.50

TRIPOD ACCESSORIES

Bridge plate.	1.50
Cine 60 quick release	2.50

Cine 60 suction cup car mount	15.00
Camera Jacks set	1.00
Geared wedge	10.00
Tilt wedge	5.00
Fixed wedge	3.50
Stay sets (3)	.75
Tie down chains set	1.00
Triangle	.75

BODY BRACES AND STABILIZERS

Arriflex shoulder pod	1.50
Arriflex shoulder pod with pistol grip	2.00
Arriflex pistol grip only	1.00
Arriflex BL brace	3.50
Cinekad shoulder brace	3.00
35mm Arriflex offset plate for above	1.00
F&B/Ceco Eclair NPR body harness	2.50
Kenyon KS-4 gyro stabilizer	10.00
Kenyon KS-6 gyro stabilizer	20.00
Leo pod	5.00
Prenzel — double shoulder harness	3.00
Ski brace	5.00

F&B/Ceco Aero-Vision Helicopter Mount **150.00**

DOLLIES AND CRANES

Moviola crab dolly with side boards and 9″ riser	35.00
Moviola crab low boom with weights	10.00
Moviola offset plate or extension tongue	10.00
Colortran crab dolly with side boards, 2-CO_2 bottles, 9″ riser	35.00
Spare CO_2 bottle	7.50
Colortran dolly low head mount	3.50
Elemack leveling head for Colortran dolly	7.50
Fisher crab dolly with six running boards	35.00
Western dolly — 4 wheel platform:	
Large with pneumatic tires	18.00
Medium with pneumatic tires	18.00
Small with hard tires	15.00
Porta dolly with electric pump	25.00
3 wheel collapsible bike dolly	10.00
Sputnick, hydraulic tripod dolly	15.00
3 wheel folding triangle dolly	3.50
Dolly hi hats	5.00
Dolly U Channel track, per foot	.25

ELEMACK

4 or 8 wheel Spyder dolly	35.00
Steel tracking wheels, per set	10.00
Straight or curved pipe track — per section	5.00
Offset low boy	5.00
Mini Jib arm with weights	35.00
3 wheel collapsible hydraulic dolly	15.00
3 wheel crab hydraulic dolly	15.00

CRANES

Chapman "Electra" 12′	75.00
Chapman "Atlas" 17′	125.00

NOTE: Transportation charge additional for Electra
crane. Driver necessary for Atlas crane.

FILTERS

STANDARD COLORS, ND or COMBINATIONS
2 x 2	.50
3 x 3	.75
4 x 4	1.50
5 x 5	2.50
Series 5 through 9	1.00
10 x 25	2.00
6 x 20	2.50

FOGS, DIFFUSION or POLARIZERS
2 x 2	.75
3 x 3	1.00
4 x 4	2.00
5 x 5	3.50
Series 5 through 9	1.50
10 x 25	3.00
6 x 20	3.50

STAR
2 x 2	5.00
3 x 3	7.50
Series 5 through 9	10.00
10 x 25	12.50
6 x 20	15.00

PROXARS
Series 5 through 9	1.25
10 x 25	2.50
6 x 20	3.00

EXPOSURE METERS
Spectra professional	5.00
Honeywell or Minolta spot	10.00
High speed meter	10.00
Underwater Weston	10.00
Weston, Norwood, or G.E.	1.50
Weston 756	6.00
Weston 614 foot candle meter with multiplier	5.00
Spectra 2 color meter	10.00
Spectra 3 color meter with filter	15.00

FINDERS
Directors Tewe or Intercinema	2.50
Dual finder attachment	3.50
Open sight finder	6.00
Monocular finder	10.00
Mitchell finder	5.00
Mitchell wide angle adapter	1.00
BNC periscope	10.00
Arriflex periscope	7.50
Eclair erect image finder	7.50

MISCELLANEOUS CAMERA ACCESSORIES
6 image rotating prism	12.50
Siamese battery cable	1.00
Hot plate 110v AC-DC	7.50
Triangle with clamps	.75
Changing bag	.75
Slate with clapsticks	.50
Dummy TV camera with lenses	30.00
Variable anamorphic	30.00
Intervalometer	10.00

```
Stop watch ........................................    .75
Front surface mirror with bracket................  10.00
Lens adaptors: Arri to "C" mount ................   1.75
             Arri to Eclair .......................   1.75
             Mark II to BNC-R ....................   3.00
             "C" to 16 Mitchell ...................   1.50
             "S" to "C"...........................   1.50
Gel cutter for Mark II ...........................   5.00
Wide angle converter for 90mm macro............   5.00
```

POWER SUPPLIES — REGULATORS — CONVERTERS

```
6 or 12v auto battery ............................   5.00
Battery charger.................................   1.50
Frezzolini 100D AC inverter 100 watts............  20.00
          100DC (crystal) AC inverter 100 watts.......  40.00
          1000DX AC inverter 35 watts .............  25.00
          1000DXC (crystal) AC inverter .............  50.00
Extra 1000DX or DXC battery......................   7.50
Inverter: 275 watt AC from 12v DC .................  10.00
Rotary Converters: 110v AC 60 cycle output:
          12v DC input 200 watt ......................  15.00
          24v DC input 500 watt ......................  30.00
          48v DC input 750 watt ......................  40.00
          48v DC input 1500 watt 110v and 230v 3 phase ..  90.00
Reverter to use 220 3 phase motor from 110v source ...  15.00
Reverter-regulator (transistorized) combination unit ...  25.00
Voltage regulator 110v AC........................  10.00
Voltage regulator 220v AC 3 phase................  12.50
```

SOUND EQUIPMENT

1/4" TAPE RECORDERS

Daily

NAGRA III with sync head, ATN, Beyer headset,
  lavalier, 666 or D24E mike, case 35.00
NAGRA III as above with crystal sync generator 50.00

NAGRA IVL with sync head, built in camera speed
  indicator, self resolver, ATN, Beyer headset,
  lavalier, 666 or D24E mike, case 50.00
NAGRA IVL as above with crystal sync generator 65.00

NAGRA ACCESSORIES

```
ATN AC sync power supply ......................   5.00
BMT 4 channel mixer .............................  12.50
BS preamplifier.................................   5.00
DH playback amplifier / speaker ..................   7.50
SV speed adjuster...............................   5.00
SLO playback synchronizer ......................  15.00
SQS crystal sync generator ......................  15.00
Jensen-crystal sync generator....................  15.00
Beyer DT 48 headset ...........................   2.50
```

AEROVOX-TANDBERG

  with sync head, 2-mike input, headset, power
  supply, lavalier, 666 or D24E mike................. 35.00

STELLAVOX

  with sync head, headset, power supply, lavalier,
  666 or D24E mike 35.00

SONY CASSETTE RECORDER with mike 5.00
WOLLENSAK, monaural recorder with mike 7.50

MICROPHONE MIXERS
Altec 342B, 4 channel. 15.00
Altec 1592A, 5 channel. 20.00
Nagra BMT, 4 channel 12.50
Shure M68 with AC power supply 15.00

MICROPHONES
Sennheiser 404, 804 or 815 with TM 515, KAT-11,
     battery pack, windscreen, shock mount and case   15.00
Sennheiser MD-214 lavalier 5.00
Electrovoice RE-15 super cardioid 5.00
Electrovoice 642, shotgun with windscreen and
    shock mount 10.00
Electrovoice 643, super dynamic 50.00
Electrovoice 635A, 649B, 654, 655 or 666 . . . .   5.00
Electrovoice 668 dynamic cardiod 12.50
RCA BK6B or BK12A lavalier 5.00
RCA BK1A, BK5A, 44BX, 77DX 5.00
RCA KU3A, (10001) Hi output ribbon. 10.00
RCA 10006 directional condenser 10.00
AKG, D24E, D25 . . . .   5.00
Altec 639B lavalier 5.00
Audio Ltd. wireless system 35.00
Sennheiser wireless system 35.00
Vega wireless system 35.00

MICROPHONE ACCESSORIES
Pigtail adapters — XL, UA, P, etc. 25
Phasing cable 25
Desk stand 50
Floor stand 1.00
Hangers and shock mounts . . . . from   .50
Mike extension cable . . . . per foot   .02
Windscreens. . . . . from   .50
Snap off adapters . . . . from   .50
Electrovoice 513 cut off filter. 1.00
Sennheiser MZA-6 battery pack 50
Sennheiser MZF-4 low Z cut off filter 1.00
Sennheiser MZN-4/1 AC power supply. 1.00

MICROPHONE BOOMS
Fisher 19' with perambulator 25.00
Mole-Richardson with perambulator 20.00
Atlas with stand 10.00
F&B/Ceco fishpole with stand 7.50

MISCELLANEOUS SOUND EQUIPMENT
Playback amplifier with enclosed speaker 7.50
Loud hailer or bull horn 5.00
Walkie-talkies (per pair). 15.00
Headsets 2.50
Altec P.A. amplifier 342B 15.00
Altec P.A. amplifier 1592A (AC or battery). 20.00
Column speakers 10.00
16" Studio speaker. 15.00
12" Outdoor speaker 15.00
Altec A7 speaker system 25.00
Speaker-50' extension cable 1.00
Dummy TV camera with lenses and tripod 35.00
Tape degausser, pencil type 1.00

Tape degausser, bulk type.......................... 5.00
Tape degausser, semi automatic bulk type............. 10.00
Audio patch cables .... from   25
Camera sync cables 1.50

VIDEO TAPE RECORDERS AND CLOSED CIRCUIT TV (CCTV)

	Daily	Weekly
CCTV-1		
Includes: one camera, 25mm lens, 8″ monitor and 16′ camera cable............	25.00	75.00
CCTV-2		
Includes: one camera, 25mm lens, 8″ monitor, 16′ camera cable, microphone, 10′ microphone cable and desk stand	30.00	90.00
CCTV-3		
Includes: one camera, 25mm lens, viewfinder for camera, 8″ monitor, 16′ camera cable, microphone, 10′ microphone cable and desk stand ..:........................	40.00	120.00
CCTV-4		
Includes: one camera, fl.8 20-80mm zoom lens, viewfinder for camera, 8″ monitor, 16′ camera cable, microphone, 10′ microphone cable and desk stand	55.00	165.00

SONY VIDEO TAPE RECORDERS	Daily	Weekly
AV 3600 1/2″ VTR........................	50.00	150.00
CV 2200 1/2″ VTR duplicator deck	60.00	180.00
AV 5000 1/2″ VTR color deck...............	125.00	375.00

LOCATION CCTV-ROVER		
Portable battery powered Sony Rover camera, recorder, built in 1 hr. battery, tripod, pistol grip, AC adapter, 16-64mm zoom lens and built in 1″ monitor. Total weight of camera and recorder is 21 pounds...............	100.00	300.00
Extra 1 hr. battery pack	2.00	6.00
Extra 3 hr. battery pack	6.00	18.00

TV RECEIVER/MONITORS		
8″ (measured diagonally)	9.00	27.00
11″ (measured diagonally)	12.00	36.00
18″ (measured diagonally)	15.00	45.00

ACCESSORIES		
CMA-1 deck adapter to use AVC 3400 camera with AV3600 videodeck.................	3.50	10.50
TV to VTR adapter.......................	3.00	9.00
Monitor to deck cable	1.00	3.00
Y or branch cables.......................	.75	2.25
Elevator tripod	2.50	7.50

CAMERA CABLES		
CCF-10, 32′ extension....................	1.00	3.00
CCF-25, 82′ extension....................	2.50	7.50
CCF-50, 164′ extension...................	4.50	13.50

CO-AX CAMERA CABLES

RGC-5, 5' extension	.50	1.50
RGC-15, 15' extension	.75	2.25
RGC-25, 25' extension	1.50	4.50
RGC-50, 50' extension	2.50	7.50
RGC-100, 100' extension	5.00	15.00

LENSES

5.7, 5.9 or 8mm	10.00	40.00
10mm to 152mm	5.00	20.00
Zoom lens 20mm to 80mm	15.00	45.00
Zoom lens 16mm to 64mm	15.00	45.00
Zoom lens 15mm to 150mm	30.00	120.00

THE FOLLOWING ITEMS AVAILABLE FOR PURCHASE ONLY

V-30F Video tape, 5" reel, 380' — 10 min	9.95
V-30D Video tape, 5" reel, 845' — 20 min	14.95
V-30H Video tape, 5-1/8" reel, 1210' — 30 min	21.95
V-30 Video tape, 7" reel, 380' — 10 min	9.95
V-31 Video tape, 7" reel, 1240' — 30 min	21.95
V-32 Video tape, 7" reel, 2370' — 60 min	39.95
RH-7V, 7" empty reel, for V-32, — 60 min	2.95
RH-5V, 5" empty reel, for V-30D, — 20 min	2.75
RH-72V, 7" empty reel, for V-30, V-31, — 30 min	2.95

EDITING

MOVIOLAS

NOTE: 16mm and 35mm sound or picture heads are interchangeable, please specify when ordering.

	Daily	Weekly	Monthly
BASIC MOVIOLA: 1 composite optical sound and picture head plus 1 optical and magnetic sound head with reel arms	-	75.00	150.00
BASIC MOVIOLA EQUIPPED WITH:			
1 additional sound head, add	-	20.00	50.00
2 additional sound heads, add	-	60.00	160.00
3 additional sound heads, add	-	80.00	225.00
1 additional picture head, add	-	35.00	100.00
2 additional picture heads, add	-	-	330.00
Table top Moviola — silent picture head only	10.00	40.00	100.00
Moviola search head	10.00	40.00	100.00

MOVIOLA ACCESSORIES

	Daily	Weekly	Monthly
Picture head only	15.00	60.00	150.00
Sound head only	7.50	30.00	75.00
Extension plate only	5.00	20.00	50.00
Headsets	1.00	4.00	10.00
TV or 1.85-1 Mask rented separately	.25	1.00	2.50
Cinemascope attachment	1.00	4.00	10.00
Film bag with hoop	.50	2.00	5.00

FILM VIEWERS

	Daily	Weekly	Monthly
F&B/Ceco 16mm or 35mm (4" x 6" screen)	5.00	20.00	50.00

F&B/Ceco 16mm or 35mm
with footage counter	6.00	24.00	60.00
with optical sound reader	7.50	30.00	75.00
16mm Zeiss Moviscop...................	2.50	10.00	25.00
Moviola 16mm........................	5.00	20.00	50.00
Super 8.............................	3.00	12.00	30.00

SYNCHRONIZERS
NOTE: Prices shown are for choice of 16mm
or 35mm. Combination 16/35, add
.50¢ to daily rate. Please specify
when ordering.

Footage counters are standard
equipment on all synchronizers.
Frame or second counters available instead for most models at
added cost.

1 or 2 gang	2.00	8.00	20.00
3 or 4 gang	3.00	12.00	30.00
6 gang...............................	5.00	20.00	50.00
Magnetic head attachment...............	1.00	4.00	10.00
Amplifier with enclosed speaker	2.00	8.00	20.00
Mixer 1 to 4 inputs.....................	1.00	4.00	10.00
70mm 1 gang	2.00	8.00	20.00

REWINDS
Single, double or 4 reel, clamp or bolt on,
per pair	2.00	8.00	20.00
Mounted on formica board, add	.50	2.00	5.00
Swivel base for rewind	.50	2.00	5.00
Differential, 2-way, each.................	5.00	20.00	50.00
Differential, 4-way, each................	9.00	36.00	90.00
Power rewind, with feed rewind on board...	10.00	40.00	100.00

NOTE: No charge for spacers and locks
when ordered with rewinds.

FILM SPLICERS (CEMENT)
Griswold, 16mm or 35mm	.50	2.00	5.00
Maier-Hancock 8/16mm.................	2.50	10.00	25.00
Maier-Hancock 8/Super 8/16mm	3.50	14.00	35.00
Maier-Hancock 16/35mm................	4.50	18.00	45.00

FILM SPLICERS (TAPE)
Rivas, HFC, Acmade or Guillotine
(16mm or 35mm)	2.50	10.00	25.00

MISCELLANEOUS EDITING EQUIPMENT
Sound reader 16mm/35mm
optical or magnetic....................	5.00	20.00	50.00
optical and magnetic	8.00	32.00	80.00
Electrical footage counter			
16mm or 35mm	1.50	6.00	15.00
combination 16/35mm	2.00	8.00	20.00
Stop watch...........................	.75	3.00	7.50
Film barrel with liner...................	1.50	6.00	15.00
Pin rack for film barrel	.50	2.00	5.00
Formica top editing table, with light well....	-	10.00	30.00
Back rack	-	2.00	5.00

Editing stool..........................				2.00	5.00
Reels to 2000'		.15		.50	1.50
Split reel to 1200"....................		.50		2.00	5.00
Punch-number or cue..................		.50		2.00	5.00
Bloop		.50		2.00	5.00
Flange...............................		.75		3.00	7.50

LIGHTING

Bulbs not included. Rates upon request.

INCANDESCENT SPOTLIGHTING

	Inky	750/ 1000w	2K	5K	10K	Big Eye 10K
Head and stand	1.25	2.00	3.50	4.50	10.00	11.00
Barndoor	.30	.75	1.00	1.25	1.50	2.50
Scrim	.15	.30	.45	.60	.90	1.25
Gel frame	.15	.30	.45	.60	.90	1.25
Snoot (each)	.20	.25	.35	.50	.70	
Ted Lewis	.30	.30				
Clamp	.35	.35	.45	.45	1.00	1.00
Stand	.75	.75	1.25	1.50	2.50	2.50
Side arm	.50	.50	.50			
Sled		.45	.75	3.00	3.00	
Trombone		.60	1.25			
Pigeon wall plate	.40	.40	.50	.50		
MacBeth		2.50	3.00	4.00	7.00	10.00
Shutter		3.50	4.25	5.00	8.00	20.00

INCANDESCENT DIFFUSED LIGHTING

	Head and Stand	Silk	Net	Glass	Diffusion Holder	Diffusion Frame
Single Broad	1.25	.40		.50		.25
Double Broad	1.50	.45		.75		.50
750 W Cone	3.50	1.00	1.00			.75
2K Cone	6.00	1.25	1.25			1.00
5K Cone	8.00	1.75	1.50			1.25
5K Skypan	5.00				1.25	1.00
10K Skypan	7.50					
1/2 or full Quad	1.25	1.00			.75	.75
TV Scoop	1.50					

Daily

Quadrant.. .35
Stack spud...................................... .30

ARC LIGHTS
NOTE: RENTAL PRICES DO NOT INCLUDE CARBONS
M-R type 450-225 amp (Brute) with stand............ 45.00

```
Brute barndoor....................................    2.50
Brute gel frame ..................................    1.25
Brute scrim ......................................    1.25
Brute shutter ....................................   20.00
AC rectifier .....................................   10.00
Carbon cans ......................................     .40
Molevator ........................................   14.00
Brute stand......................................    5.00
Extra head cable .................................    1.00
Head extension cable 25' .........................    1.00
```

COLORTRAN LIGHTING CONVERTERS
```
Junior — for 6-150W lamps or equivalent ............    3.00
Senior — for 10-150W lamps or equivalent ...........    4.00
Cinemaster Junior — for 2-500W lamps on 110v or
        3-500W lamps on 220v ......................    6.00
Cinemaster for 4-500W lamps on 110v or 7-500W
        lamps on 220v .............................    8.00
Cinemaster chief MKII same as above but with
        4 independent booster controls ...............   10.00
3 wire to 2 wire adapter ..........................     .40
```

COLORTRAN LIGHTING
```
Cine King with stand .............................    2.50
Cine Queen with stand.............................    2.50
Accessories for Cine King or Cine Queen
        barndoor...................................     .75
        gel frame.................................     .35
        scrim.....................................     .45
R80 head with stand...............................    3.50
        diffuser..................................     .60
        barndoor..................................    1.00
```

QUARTZ LIGHTING

COLORTRAN OR BARDWELL & McALISTER
```
650W Mini Pro Head................................    3.00
650W Dual with yoke and stand ....................    2.50
650W Dual with medium screw base .................    2.50
650W Focusing Multi beam with stand...............    3.00
650W Mini Mac or Mini light broad with
        barndoors and stand .......................    2.25
Barndoor and accessory holder for 650's ..........     .75
Single or double scrim for 650's .................     .30
Dichroic filter for 650's.........................    2.50
1000W Focusing Multi beam with stand..............    3.50
1000W Focusing Vari beam with stand...............    3.50
1000W Dual Quartz King with stand.................    3.00
1000W Dual Quartz King with screw base ...........    3.00
500-1000 Wide flood head with stand ..............    3.00
1000W Variable broad with stand...................    3.50
1000W True broad with stand.......................    3.50
Barndoor and accessory holder for 1000's .........     .75
Single or double scrim for 1000's ................     .35
Diffusion frame for 1000's........................     .35
Dichroic filter for 1000's........................    3.00
Diffusion glass for broad ........................    1.00
Intensifiers .....................................    5.00
1000W Mini Mac or Mini light broad with
        barndoors and stand ......................    3.00
1000W Back light with barndoors and stand ........    3.00
```

```
1-light 21" cyc strip................................     3.00
4-light 7' cyc strip ..............................    10.00
Guard for cyc strip ..............................      .75
Hanger for cyc strip .............................      .25
2000W Double broad with stand....................     5.00
2000W Slim line pan with stand ...................     4.00
2000W Focusing spot with stand ..................     6.00
Barndoor for 2000's ..............................      .85
Single or double scrim for 2000's ................      .45
Snoot for 2000's .................................      .45
Dichroic for 2000's ..............................     5.00
```

MINI AND MAXI BRUTES
```
Mini Brute 6 light with stand.....................     6.50
      Barndoor ...................................     1.00
Mini Brute 9 light with stand ....................     9.00
      Barndoor ...................................     1.00
Maxi Brute 6 light with stand.....................    10.00
      Barndoor ...................................     1.50
Maxi Brute 9 light with stand.....................    15.00
      Barndoor ...................................     1.50
```

MOLE-RICHARDSON
```
650W Nook light with yoke, barndoor and stand ........  2.25
      Single or double scrim......................      .30
      Diffusion frame ............................      .30
      Right angle spud adapter ...................      .30
      Handle .....................................      .30
      3 light yoke ...............................      .75
650W Teenie Mole with stand ......................     2.25
      Barndoor and accessory holder ..............      .75
      Single or double scrim......................      .30
      Diffusion frame ............................      .30
      Dichroic filter ............................     2.50
1000W Mickey Mole with stand......................     3.50
      Barndoor and accessory holder ..............      .75
      Single or double scrim......................      .35
      Diffusion frame ............................      .35
      Dichroic filter ............................     3.00
1000W Molequartz Broad with stand.................     3.50
      Barndoor ...................................      .75
      Diffusion glass ............................     1.00
      Diffuser scrim holder.......................      .35
2000W Molequartz Broad with stand.................     5.00
      Barndoor ...................................     1.00
      Diffusion glass ............................     1.25
      Diffusion scrim holder .....................      .50
2000W Mighty Mole with stand......................     6.00
      Barndoor ...................................      .85
      Single or double scrim......................      .45
      Diffusion frame ............................      .45
      Dichroic filter ............................     5.00
      Snoot.......................................      .45
```

FAY LIGHTS
```
1-light Fay.......................................     1.25
2-light Fay.......................................     2.50
      Barndoor and holder ........................     1.00
      Silk .......................................      .75
      Diffusion frame ............................      .75
5 light Fay.......................................     5.00
9-light Fay.......................................    10.00
      Barndoor ...................................     1.00
```

Silk 2.00
Diffusion frame 2.00

SOFT LIGHTS
750W with stand................................ 3.50
  Silk 1.00
  Diffusion frame .... .75
1000W with stand............................... 3.50
  Silk 2.00
  Diffusion frame 1.00
2000W with stand............................... 7.00
2000W light weight with stand 7.50
  Silk 2.00
  Diffusion frame 1.00
4000W with stand............................... 12.50
  Silk 2.50
  Diffusion frame 1.50
8000W with stand............................... 14.50
  Silk 2.50
  Diffusion frame 1.50

SPECIAL PURPOSE LIGHTING
Lowell K-5 kit 3.00
Lowell Uni 6 kit 5.00
Lowell lights (individually) with barndoors .... .75
Lowell light barndoors and clips only .... .45
Gator grip with socket .... .45
Gator grip barndoors .... .45
Pic stand .... .50
Obie light with camera bracket and 2 silks............ 6.00
Strip light — 7 Bulb 7′ 3.50
          9 Bulb 9′ 4.00
        14 Bulb 14′ 5.00
750W Leko with hanger.......................... 12.50
30v Sungun head with battery 12.50
30v Battery only 7.50
Dichroic for sungun 1.25

FOLLOW SPOTS
650W quartz Trouperette 15.00
1000W quartz Colortran 15.00
2000W Molenser................................ 15.00
3000W Dynabeam 20.00
5000W Dynabeam 30.00
A.C. Trouper (carbon arc) 45.00
A.C. Super Trouper (carbon arc).................. 85.00
NOTE: All follow spots supplied with bulb, color changer,
     iris and stand. Carbons are purchase only.

MISCELLANEOUS LIGHTING ACCESSORIES
Clip on barndoors.............................. .20
Italian gooseneck .... .50
Barndoors for above............................ .20
Gaffer grip with stud .... .30
750W foco spot 3.50
750W side arm bracket .... .50
750W TV hanger................................ 1.25
750W double hanging pigeon .... .60
750W pigeon................................... .40
750W double header .... .50

```
750W triple header.....................................  .60
750W pipe clamp .....................................  .35
750W adjustable claw ................................  .60
750W trombone ......................................  .60
2KW pipe clamp .....................................  .45
2KW side arm bracket ...............................  .50
2KW TV hanger......................................  1.50
2KW pigeon..........................................  .50
2KW trombone ......................................  1.25
2KW trapeze ........................................  .85
2KW spot arm with adapter..........................  .90
      adapter only....................................  .30
2KW sled ...........................................  .80
T Bone turtle........................................  .75
2K set wall bracket..................................  .60
2K extension arm ...................................  .60
2K spot jack.........................................  .75
```

LIGHTING STANDS

```
Light weight or PIC stands..........................  .75
750W aluminum regular or high .....................  .75
750W regular or low.................................  .75
750W stand riser ...................................  .50
750W sky hi.........................................  1.00
2KW regular or low..................................  1.25
2KW stand riser ....................................  .50
2KW sky hi..........................................  1.50
5KW regular or low..................................  1.25
5KW sky hi..........................................  1.50
10KW...............................................  1.50
Duarc stand.........................................  2.00
Brute stand.........................................  3.00
Crank up stand .....................................  3.50
Molevator ..........................................  14.00
Hydra lift — AC-DC..................................  14.00
Molevator dolly.....................................  25.00
750W Boom stand ..................................  3.00
Pole cat — to 7' ....................................  1.00
Pole cat — to 11'...................................  1.25
Pole cat — to 15'...................................  1.50
Cross bars 4'-8' ....................................  .30
Cross bar fittings ...................................  .15
24" iron bases ......................................  3.00
1-1/2" black threaded pipe-per section .............  3.00
Cheesebros 1-1/2" right angle or swivel.............  .60
Hand rail bear trap..................................  2.50
Meat ax ............................................  1.25
```

REFLECTORS

```
30 x 36 with stand and yoke........................  4.50
48 x 48 with stand and yoke........................  5.50
42 x 42 aluminum with stand and yoke..............  7.00
20 x 24 aluminum ..................................  4.50
Book reflector ......................................  3.00
Lowell 2 x 2 Variflector with stand .................  3.00
Lowell 4 x 4 Variflector with stand .................  5.00
Reflector stand only .................................  1.50
Ground rod .........................................  .30
Reflector net .......................................  1.50
```

COLORTRAN ELECTRONIC QUARTZ DIMMERS

```
650W mini dyne .....................................  1.50
1000W mini dyne ....................................  2.00
1000W color dyne...................................  2.75
```

```
2000W color dyne.............................  4.00
3000W color dyne.............................  5.50
6000W color dyne.............................  8.00
Single remote control........................   .75
Multiple (6) remote control ..................  3.50
Mastering remote control ....................  4.00
Remote control cable 25'.....................   .35
                     50' .....................   .70
                    100' .....................  1.40
                    200' .....................  2.80
```

DIMMERS
```
2000W........................................  2.50
3000W........................................  3.00
5000W........................................  5.00
10,000W......................................  12.00
```

VARIACS — AC ONLY
```
7-1/2 amp....................................  1.75
7-1/2 amp with meter.........................  4.00
15 amp.......................................  2.50
15 amp with meter ...........................  5.00
30 amp.......................................  5.00
50 amp.......................................  7.50
90 amp.......................................  15.00
```
NOTE: Variacs and dimmers supplied with case,
      feeder, cable and outlet box.

DIMMER BANKS
```
4-2000W with master..........................  20.00
4-5000W with master..........................  30.00
12-5000W with master.........................  60.00
```

CABLES
```
4/0 single conductor feeder cable.............. per ft.   .04
2/0 or #2 single conductor feeder cable.......... per ft.   .03
4/0 or 2/0 single jumper .........................   .50
2 wire stage cable............................ per ft.   .04
3 wire stage cable............................ per ft.   .05
4 wire stage cable............................ per ft.   .06
2 wire 12/2 or 16/2 Hubbell extension.......... per ft.   .02
3 phase camera cable — twist lock.............. per ft.   .04
25 amp single pocket extension   — 25'................  1.00
                                 — 50'................  1.75
60 amp single pocket extension   — 25'................  1.25
                                 — 50'................  2.00
100 amp single pocket extension — 25'................  1.50
100 amp double pocket extension — 25'................  1.50
Cable winder..................................  7.50
```

TIE-INS
```
Single tie-in 2/0 or 4/0 with lugs...................   .40
                        with clips ..................   .50
2 wire tie-in with lugs..............................   .75
              with clips.............................   .85
3 wire tie-in with lugs..............................  1.00
              with clips.............................  1.25
4 wire tie-in with lugs..............................  1.25
              with clips.............................  1.50
3 phase camera tie in................................  1.25
2 wire Hubbell tie in with clips.....................   .75
Anderson buss bar clamps.............................   .60
```

SIAMESE
```
2 wire stage.................................  1.25
```

```
3 wire stage.....................................  1.50
4 wire stage.....................................  1.75
4/0 single.......................................   .40
4/0 3-fer .......................................   .50
2/0 single.......................................   .40
2/0 3-fer .......................................   .50
```

CABLE ADAPTERS
```
301 1/2 .........................................   .35
Stage plug to tweco .............................   .50
Tweco to single pocket ..........................   .50
Tweco to double pocket ..........................   .75
Tweco to six-fer.................................   .50
Tweco to six-fer harness 6'......................  1.00
Tweco to six-fer harness 9'......................  1.00
Tweco to six-fer harness 18'.....................  1.25
Tweco to six-fer harness 24'.....................  1.50
3 wire Hubbell to 2 wire Hubbell.................   .35
Hubbell two-fers.................................   .35
Hubbell straight to twist lock...................   .35
Tweco adapters...................................   .35
M/R buss bar to Tweco............................   .35
```

BOXES
```
4 way Hubbell box................................   .85
6 or 8 way Hubbell box ..........................  1.45
3 wire 12 way Hubbell box .......................  2.00
2 wire 4 pocket plugging box ....................  1.50
2 wire 6 pocket plugging box ....................  1.50
3 wire 4 pocket plugging box ....................  2.00
3 wire 6 pocket plugging box ....................  2.00
4 wire 6 pocket plugging box ....................  3.00
```

SWITCHES AND BOARDS
```
60 amp 3 phase 4 wire bull switch................   3.00
100 amp 3 phase 4 wire bull switch ..............   4.50
200 or 300 amp 3 phase 4 wire bull switch........   5.50
400 or 500 amp 3 phase 4 wire bull switch........   7.50
600 amp 3 phase 4 wire bull switch ..............  10.00
M/R remote switch board — 3 wire.................  12.50
M/R remote switch board — 4 wire.................  15.00
```

GENERATORS

Daily
```
25 amp AC........................................   20.00
30 amp AC........................................   20.00
50 amp AC........................................   40.00
300 amp AC 3 phase on truck .....................  175.00
375 amp DC on trailer ...........................  175.00
750 amp DC on truck
        first 3 hours ...........................   90.00
        each additional hour ....................   20.00
1000 amp DC on truck
        first 3 hours ...........................  120.00
        each additional hour ....................   30.00
1500 amp DC on truck
        first 3 hours ...........................  195.00
        each additional hour ....................   70.00
```

Note: Charges will be made for:
   1. Gasoline and oil
   2. Delivery on trailers
   3. Truck charges .70 per mile outside N.Y.C. limits

Operators and drivers to be supplied and paid by users, and to be approved by F & B/Ceco, Inc.

There will be a three hour minimum charge per day for each generator except on non-working Saturdays, Sundays and Holidays.

GRIP EQUIPMENT

GRIP STANDS
	Daily
M/R Century stand	1.50
Century light	1.50
Century regular	1.50
Century medium	1.75
Century medium high	1.75
Century high overhead (hi boy)	2.75
H.S.D. folding century (light weight)	1.75
Extra gobo head with double arms	.75

DIFFUSERS
12″ x 18″ single net	.50
12″ x 18″ double net	.60
18″ x 24″ single net	.70
18″ x 24″ double net	.75
24″ x 30″ single net	.90
24″ x 30″ double net	1.00
30″ x 36″ single net	1.25
30″ x 36″ double net	1.50
Diffuser box	.25

BLACK FLAGS
6″ x 10″	.40
8″ x 20″	.40
12″ x 14″	.40
18″ x 24″	.55
10″ x 36″	.55
10″ x 44″	.55
16″ x 48″	.70
16″ x 72″	.80
19″ x 48″	.70
24″ x 36″	.70
24″ x 60″	.90
24″ x 72″	1.00
30″ x 36″	1.75
36″ x 36″	2.00
36″ x 48″	2.00

DOTS AND COOKIES
Single scrim dot 4″, 6″, 8″, 10″	.25
Double scrim dot 4″, 6″, 8″, 10″	.30
Solid dot 4″, 6″, 8″, 10″	.20
Gooseneck for dots	.35
Lucite cookie	1.25
18 x 24 wood cookie	1.00
24 x 30 wood cookie	1.25
14 x 36 cello cookie	1.25
Plastic strips	.20

BOBBINETS, SILKS AND DROPS
10′ x 10′ bobbinet	7.50
12′ x 12′ bobbinet	10.00
18′ x 18′ bobbinet	15.00
20′ x 20′ bobbinet	20.00
10′ x 12′ silk	7.50

```
12' x 15' silk.....................................  10.00
12' x 15' black backdrops.........................   7.50
20' x 20' black backdrops.........................  10.00
```

BUTTERFLIES   Daily
```
6' x 6' complete with single net, double net............
              silk and solid.....................   9.00
              extra 6 x 6 net or silk ............   1.75
12' x 12' complete with single net, double net
              silk and solid.....................  15.00
```

PARALLELS
```
6' Aluminum ......................................   8.50
4' − 5' − 6' steel interlocked....................   6.50
casters for parallels set of 4 regular ...........   1.50
                         set of 4 large ..........   2.25
Hand rail ........................................   4.00
Jack riser........................................   3.50
Parallel hoist (less rope) .......................   2.50
```

C CLAMPS
```
4" or 6".......................................... .35
8" or 10" ........................................ .70
12"..............................................  1.50
4" or 6" with 750 stud............................ .60
8" or 10" with 750 stud...........................  1.25
Jorgensen clamp with 750 stud.................... .60
```

LADDERS AND BOXES
```
4' or 6' .........................................   1.00
8' ...............................................   1.50
10' ..............................................   2.00
12' ..............................................   2.50
16' ..............................................   3.00
32' extension.....................................   7.50
Apple box......................................... .25
Pancake.......................................... .25
Apple box — nest of 6.............................   3.50
Step block ....................................... .25
Donut stop block small or large.................. .20
Molevator donut.................................. .35
Wedges ........................................... .10
4' x 8' plywood sheets............................   2.50
```

MISCELLANEOUS
```
Sandbag .......................................... .35
Block and fall (rope additional) .................   3.50
Rubber mat 6'.................................... .75
Tarpaulin: small .................................   2.50
          medium.................................   3.00
          large .................................   3.75
Lead weight...................................... .50
Furniture blanket.................................   1.00
Laundry hamper...................................   1.00
Directors chair ..................................   1.00
Location umbrella.................................   1.50
Umbrella base.................................... .60
Water thermos ...................................   1.50
Coffee thermos − 5 gal...........................   4.00
Pedestal fan .....................................   3.00
18" M/R wind machine with stand .................  15.00
Wind machine ritter 64" or mole .................  55.00
Fog machine .....................................   6.50
Dry ice basket....................................   1.50
Big jet fog machine..............................  15.00
Cob web spinner..................................   6.50
```

Chapter 4
Raw Stock

The material upon which your production is recorded is referred to as raw stock. When preparing your estimate, there are three types of raw stock to take into consideration:

1. Video tape
2. Film
3. Audio or ¼-inch tape.

VIDEO TAPE

Commercial broadcast video tape is 2 inches wide. This is the actual size of the tape. Also in use are 1-inch, ¾-inch, and ½-inch tapes, but these are not regarded as broadcast quality. Minnesota Mining and Manufacturing (3M) is the chief supplier of video tape, with Fuji, under the brand name COLTAPE, being second. Since 3M was, at one point, the only manufacturer of video tape, many producers have become accustomed to using their video tape and are not aware that there are others of comparable quality on the market.

Video tape comes in reels of 30, 60, and 90 minutes, virgin or evaluated. Whenever possible specify evaluated tape. This is tape that has been run through a video tape recorder at least once to polish any rough spots or correct any imperfections. It is more expensive than virgin tape, but it is better because there are no imperfections in the tape.

How do you estimate the amount of tape to be used in your production? If you are shooting a commercial, figure 10 minutes of tape stock per scene. For example, if there are five scenes, you will need 50 minutes or, rounded off, one 60-minute reel. When shooting a show, estimate your shooting ratio; i.e, 3:1, 4:1, 5:1, etc., and that will give you an approximate idea of the amount of tape stock to be included in your budget. If you are recording on 2 VTRs simultaneously (the second one for protection back up), double your tape stock.

If you are dealing with a large production facility, it is possible to rent the protection tape instead of having to buy it. That way, once the production is completed and you are assured of having all recorded takes, the protection tape can be erased and used again. The rental price for this protection tape is one-third to one-sixth cheaper than the purchase price.

The only time you would include audio tape in a video tape estimate would be if you needed a protection tape or wanted a separate audio track. Otherwise, it is unnecessary since the sound is recorded right onto the video tape.

FILM

The film stock needed is estimated the same as video tape, except it is based on feet rather than minutes. 16mm film runs at the rate of 36 feet a minute; 35mm at the rate of 90 feet a minute. To determine the amount of raw stock to be ordered, multiply the number of minutes in your production by the shooting ratio and the applicable feet-per-minute rate, and you have the exact amount of film to be ordered. For example, if you are shooting a half-hour show in 16mm on a 10:1 ratio, it would look like this:

30 (minutes)   X   10   X   36   or 10,800 feet of film
(show length)   (ratio)   (feet per minute)

Since 400-foot rolls are normally used in 16mm, merely divide 10,800 by 400 and you know you need to order 27 rolls of film. Or, if you are using only 100-foot rolls (improbable), you would need to order 108.

The same formula applies to 35mm. Again, a half-hour show in 35mm, this time on a 7:1 ratio:

30 (minutes)   X   7   X   90   or 18,900 feet of film
(show length)   (ratio)   (feet per minute)

Since 35mm is usually sold in 1000-foot rolls, you would divide 18,900 by 1000 to determine the number of rolls for your production. Since this comes out to 18.9, you would order 19 rolls of 35mm film for this production. As a shortcut to all of this, you can figure a 400-foot roll of 16mm and a 1000-foot roll of 35mm represents approximately 10 minutes of time. Therefore, a 30-minute show, shot 10:1, would take 30 rolls of stock, either 16mm or 35mm.

From an estimating point of view, it is necessary to understand the basic technical specifications of each film type in order to know which will best meet the requirements of your production. Will you need a high-speed daylight film or one that is balanced for interior lighting? Are you shooting both indoors and outside and will you use one type of film with filters or two types? Are the types compatible? Is there enough light for the slower but higher fidelity films, or must you use a fast film? Will you have to "push it" (force develop) in the lab? A simple key to film type is the ASI rating. The lower the rating, the slower the film and the more light you will need.

Most film types are available in both 35mm and 16mm. The majority of 16mm shooting, though, is done on reversal film and most 35mm shooting is done on negative. If you shoot with negative film, an intermediate step is necessary between your original camera negative (the film you actually shoot) and the internegative from which your prints are made. This intermediate step is called an interpositive (IP) and is required because of the difficulty of printing a negative (the internegative) from another negative (the original negative) and to protect the rather fragile negative stock from damage.

The interpositive is made after editing is completed and includes only the selected scenes that are going to be used in the release print. It is not necessary to make an IP of the "outtakes." Be sure to include the price for an IP in your budget.

If your original is a positive stock, such as Ektachrome reversal, the intermediate step is not necessary. This is because it is easy to make an internegative directly from the positive original. The reversal stock is more durable than negative stock because its emulsion is harder and will stand more handling. The biggest supplier and manufacturer of professional camera and printing stock is Eastman Kodak. Others are Fuji, 3M, and Dupont.

When preparing your budget, you should understand the terminology and coding methods for each film type. As you gain expertise in budgeting, you will notice that Eastman Kodak film is seldom referred to as a specific type; usually, it is referred to by its code number. For example, a cameraman or producer will ask you to budget an equal amount of 7242 and 7252 for the production. These are 16mm reversal films; 7242 is used for interior shots having limited lighting and 7252 used for the exterior photography.

Although there are four numbers for each type of film, i.e., 7242, 7252, 5252, etc., your prime concern is with the first two numbers. Film that is 35mm or wider is part of the 5000 series; 16mm or smaller, 7000 series. Therefore, the first digit in

35mm is 5 and in 16mm 7. The second digit indicates that it is a print film or original camera-intermediate film. If the second number is 3, it indicates a print film; if 2, an original camera film or intermediate film. The last two numbers refer to the specific type of film.

The other suppliers of film do not have as many types of film available nor as simple a coding system. When Fuji film is included in a budget, it must be identified by specific name rather than code number. For example, for a 16mm production, you would have to specify "16mm Fujicolor Negative Film" rather than using their code number 8516, since the code number is the same for both 16mm and 35mm film.

AUDIO TAPE

In film, estimate how much time will be spent shooting sync sound. This will help you determine the amount of audio tape (¼-inch tape) to be included in your budget. The most commonly used tape is Scotch No. 131 in 5- or 7-inch reels. At the standard 7½ i.p.s. recording speed, a 5-inch reel lasts 15 minutes and a 7-inch reel 30 minutes. Since, on each take, the sound recorder starts before the camera does and stops after, allow enough extra tape to compensate for this. For a 35mm production, use one 5-inch reel of audio tape for each 1000 feet of film. This will give you some extra tape, but it facilitates production, since the soundman can change reels the same time as the cameraman changes film. In 16mm, use one 5-inch reel of audio tape for each 400 feet of film.

In estimating audio tape, you estimate only the amount you need for sync sound. For silent shooting, you will not run the recorder. Although there are many manufacturers of audio tape, the biggest supplier is Minnesota Mining and Manufacturing (Scotch).

SHOOTING RATIO

How do you know what shooting ratio to use? That can best be answered by knowing what you are shooting. Is it a commercial or a program? Is it in a studio or on location? Is your filming project staged or spontaneous? Seldom is a production done on a less than 4-to-1 ratio and oftentimes it is much more. If a certain shot is difficult to achieve or a special effect is not working, the ratio can be as much as 30 or 40 to 1. This is common in commercial production. In fact, commercials can run as high as 100 to 1! In your preliminary estimates, use a 10:1 ratio. This is a realistic figure and will hold true for the majority of your productions. As you gain expertise in estimating and production techniques, you will be able to make a more accurate projection, depending on the type of production, the director, time involved, etc.

The most important step, then, in estimating all raw stock is the determination of your shooting ratio and what you will be shooting. Once this has been determined, it is a simple arithmetic exercise to estimate the costs for raw stock.

Chapter 5

Laboratory Charges

Unless you are using film as part of your video tape production, there are no laboratory charges with video tape. In film, though, the laboratory is a vital part of your production from the first shooting day through release prints. In order to give visual continuity to your production, it is advisable to use the same lab for the entire production. This way, if any problems arise, the responsibility has not been diffused because a number of labs were used.

Labs perform a variety of operations, all chargeable. Once the camera raw stock has been exposed, it must be sent to the lab for developing and printing. The purchase order to the lab must be highly detailed, since they will do only as they have been instructed—no more. This PO should contain your name, address, and telephone number, type of film used, title of production, the manner in which the shooting was done, the approximate footage, and details as to developing, printing, coding (edge numbering), etc. Some labs provide camera report pads so that this information gets to them in proper order (Fig. 5-1).

Not all labs offer all services. Some labs process only 16mm; others only 35mm. Some only have facilities for black and white; others both color and black and white. Before making a decision on the lab you are going to use, make sure they are equipped to handle your particular production needs.

DEVELOPING

The first lab process the film goes through is developing. The exposed camera stock is processed in a darkroom and the result is called the original (it may be a negative or positive image, depending on the type of film used). The charges for developing are based on footage and usually all production footage is developed. This is the original from which your workprint is made.

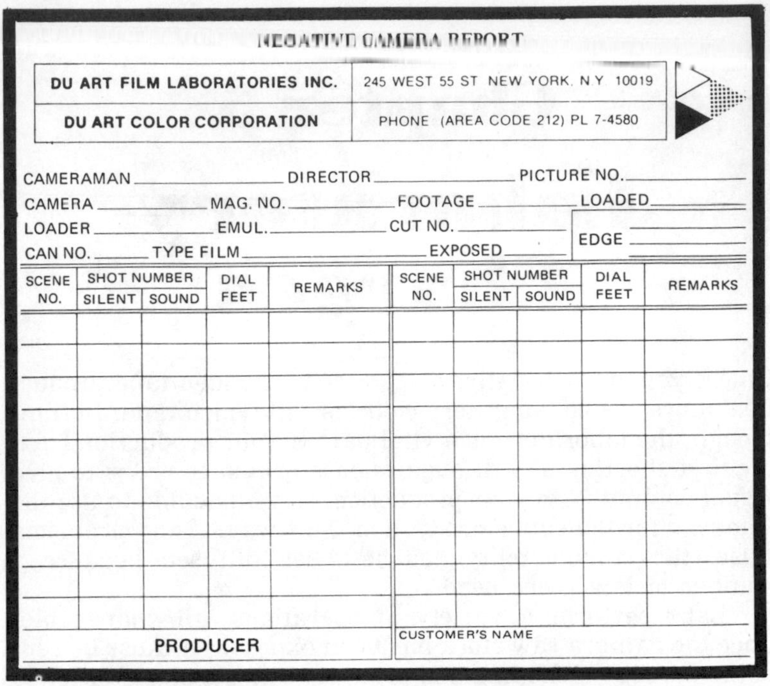

NEGATIVE CAMERA REPORT

DU ART FILM LABORATORIES INC.	245 WEST 55 ST NEW YORK, N.Y. 10019
DU ART COLOR CORPORATION	PHONE (AREA CODE 212) PL 7-4580

CAMERAMAN ______ DIRECTOR ______ PICTURE NO. ______
CAMERA ______ MAG. NO. ______ FOOTAGE ______ LOADED ______
LOADER ______ EMUL. ______ CUT NO. ______ EDGE ______
CAN NO. ______ TYPE FILM ______ EXPOSED ______

SCENE NO.	SHOT NUMBER SILENT	SHOT NUMBER SOUND	DIAL FEET	REMARKS	SCENE NO.	SHOT NUMBER SILENT	SHOT NUMBER SOUND	DIAL FEET	REMARKS

PRODUCER ______ CUSTOMER'S NAME ______

Fig. 5-1. Negative camera report form.

During the developing stage, the lab can do some correction of the film. If it has been underexposed, for example, the lab can hold the film in the developing bath longer than required. This is called forced processing or "pushing it." In this situation the color is sometimes compromised. Forced processing also is chargeable on a per-foot basis.

Not all footage that has been developed, though, need be printed. Using the camera report as a guide, the lab will print only the "takes" indicated. Printing is also charged on a per-foot basis. Some labs have a minimum charge, so if you have short reels or a small amount of footage, there will be a minimum charge instead of a footage charge. (At the end of this chapter are excerpts from a typical lab rate card.)

PRINTING

When printing your selected takes, you get a "one-lite" print unless otherwise specified. This means the lab has selected one optimum exposure for the whole print without taking time to balance density and-or color on a scene-to-scene basis. These one-lite prints are called dailies or rushes. Timed dailies are available if requested but are more expensive. Usually, timing (color balancing) is done at a later stage.

Coding or edge numbering is frequently done to assist in editing. This consists of matching sequential numbers printed along the edge of the film and corresponding sound track. This is done after sound and picture have been "matched" or put into sync. This differs from the latent edge numbers that already exist on most original stock and which print through to your workprint, an edited one-lite print with all opticals, fades, dissolves, etc., indicated, ready for negative cutting. Coding is charged on a per-foot basis and applies to both picture and track. When the workprint has been completed and the original must be cut, the edge numbers make the job of matching that much easier.

Although some laboratories offer editing facilities on an hourly basis, this is usually done by an editor or editing house (see Chapter 12). At this point there are no more lab charges until you have a completed workprint and are ready to have your original cut, print timed, and an optical negative or internegative made.

FINAL PROCESSES

Once your production has been edited, you have two options. If there are optical effects, they are shot by an optical house (see Chapter 13). Anything other than dissolves, fades, and some title work must be done that way. The majority of commercials and films have an optical negative shot of the entire film. This negative includes all scenes with titles, fades, dissolves, blowups, as well as any other special optical effects. This can be quite expensive, especially if the film is long. An alternative would be to shoot only the special opticals of the film and splice them into the original footage. The selected original footage is cut into A and B rolls which are printed together to form an internegative, or printed with the sound track to form a composite print.

If no opticals are included in your production, the next step after editing is negative cutting. Negative cutting is chargeable on an hourly basis or on a per-reel basis. Negative cutters base their rates on 10-minute reels. For productions shorter than 10 minutes, the charges are based on an hourly rate. The amount of time needed to cut your original depends on the complexity of your production and the number of scenes to be used. Always include a minimum of $50 for negative cutting and matching

Now the film goes to the lab for processing again. Fades and dissolves (the only opticals that can be done in a lab) are incorporated into the production. These are charged on a flat per-effect basis. A slop print is ordered to check all the opticals. This is the same as a one-lite print. Then the print is timed. A timer takes each scene and balances it to reflect, as accurately as possible, the scene as it was originally shot. Timing can be done manually or electronically. After the film has been timed, it is printed. This is called an answer print. This is usually more expensive than a release print because it includes the charges for timing. Usually, you get one answer print and up to three corrected prints for the initial A/P price. Again, there is a minimum charge for short lengths; otherwise, answer prints are estimated on footage. Once you have approved the A/P, an internegative is made. This is an exact copy of the original and is used for duplicating purposes. It leaves your original protected and, if the internegative is ripped or scratched, you have not lost your production because you still have the original. The internegatives are charged on a per foot basis.

There is a difference in prices, depending upon whether you are making contact prints or reduction (optical) prints. Contact prints are merely a mirror image of the original and refers to both 16mm and 35mm. Reduction prints can be 16mm prints made from a 35mm negative, 16mm prints blown up to 35mm, 16mm blown up to Super 16mm, etc. Reduction printing is more expensive than contact printing, since it is done optically rather than on a 1-to-1 ratio.

Once your production is finished, notify the lab as to the disposition of your negative material. If they are not told to dispose of it or return it, there will be a monthly storage charge.

Miscellaneous lab charges must be considered, too. These include leader, cores, reels, cans, cases, etc. Be sure that these items are included in your budget if you are asking the lab to provide them.

The labs do not provide free delivery service nor do they assume responsibility for your film when it is in the lab. You must carry your own insurance (see Chapter 14). Also, include delivery or messenger charges in your estimate for carrying the film to and from the lab.

Labs perform a number of functions. If you shoot in 16mm, they can blow it up to 35mm. Conversely, they can reduce 35mm to 16mm. The film can be made lighter or darker. Scenes can be lengthened or shortened by selected printing. Some labs handle only developing and printing of dailies.

Others are full-service facilities offering, in addition to the lab services, editing, sound transfers, distribution, negative cutting, and synchronizing. These lab charges are based on either an hourly or on a footage basis.

The major services of a lab, then, are developing, printing, coding, negative cutting, and timing. In addition, some labs offer other production services such as distribution, transfers, syncing, etc. Basic lab rates are on a footage basis or an hourly basis, depending on the service. Do not hesitate to consult with the lab you are planning on using when preparing your estimate. The advice is free and will help you prepare a more accurate budget for your film. The following pages were taken from the Du Art Film Laboratories (New York) price list.

35MM EASTMANCOLOR

	Price Per Foot
RUSHES OR DAILIES	
Develop Original Negative or Intermediate	.0616
Develop Reversal Internegative (#5249)	*
Develop Forced Processing .... Add	.026
One-Light Print	.1377
Timed Uncorrected Print	.1698
Subsequent Corrected Print (Color and Density)	.1377
Black and White Print (From Color Negative)	.0648

Note: Quality of color negative cannot be determined from black and white print.

	Price Per Foot
INTERPOSITIVES AND MASTERS	
From Color Negative (Not Previously Timed by Du Art) .... M/C $25.00	.5509
From Color Negative (Previously Timed and Corrected by Du Art) .... M/C $25.00	.4209
Black and White Pan Master (#5235) From Color Negative	.1377
Black and White Separation Pan Masters (Blue, Green, Red) Set of Three ..... M/C $40.00	.6205
From Color Interpositive (Type 5249)	*
A and B Roll .... Add	.06
Additional Roll .... Add	.06
Cord to Cord......... M/C per roll $25.00 Add	.107

	Price Per Foot
INTERNEGATIVES	
From Color Positive .... M/C $25.00	.4209
From Color Interpositive .... M/C $25.00	.4209
From Black and White Separations .... M/C $40.00	.6205
From Color Negative (Reversal Stock #5249)	*
Blow Up From 16mm Single Run to 35mm (Per 35mm Ft.)	.50
A and B Roll......... Add	.06
Additional Roll .... Add	.06
Minimum Charge Blow Up	$50.00
Cord To Cord......... M/C per roll $25.00 Add	.107

	Price Per Foot
RELEASE PRINTS (SUBJECTS 500 FEET OR OVER)	
Check Print From Internegative (Made By Du Art)	.1377
First Trial Answer Print	.4001
Single Print Order	.1090
2–10 Print Order	.0895
11–25 Print Order	.0819
26–75 Print Order	.0795
76 and Over	*
A and B Roll .... Add	.0572
Additional Roll .... Add	.0572
Cord to Cord......... M/C per roll $15.00 Add	.107

*Prices On Request

TV SPOTS (ANY LENGTH) AND SMALL ROLLS (UNDER 500 FEET)	Price Per Foot

First Trial Answer Print – First 120 Feet of Cut 0.3530
    All Additional Footage .... .4704

SUBSEQUENT PRINTING

Up to 1000 Feet .... Per Negative M/C $16.00   .1664
1,001 to 2,000 Feet .... Per Negative   .1446
2,001 to 6,000 Feet .... Per Negative   .1290
6,001 Feet and Over .... Per Negative   .1175

When laboratory is required to break down timed negative containing more than one TV Spot, there will be no charge for negative labor, but there will be a $7.50 charge per spot for printing set up.

FILMSTRIPS

Negative Developing and Color Corrected First Trial Answer Prints Three Densities
    Maximum Length 25 Feet $16.50
Up to 2,000 Feet .... Per Subject   .1430
2,001 to 5,000 Feet .... Per Subject   .1216
5,001 to 25,000 Feet .... Per Subject   .1075
Over 25,000 Feet .... Per Subject   .0995
Breaking down, canning, and attaching labels supplied by customer ....   .12 per strip

MISCELLANEOUS

Fades (First Printing Only) .... $3.50 each
Dissolves (First Printing Only) .... $7.00 each
Short Scene Printing .... Add   .006
Unspliced Raw Stock .... Add   .015
Superimposed Titles .... Add   .012

Thread-Up Waste — Add 3% to Negative Footage — Minimum 8 Feet Per Item

Minimum Charge $11.00 Per Item Except Where Noted

16MM EASTMANCOLOR

DEVELOPING

	Price Per Foot
Develop Original Negative or Intermediate	.0616
Develop Forced Processing .... Add	.026
Develop Reversal Internegative (#7249)	*

PRINT OF DAILIES OR RUSHES

	Contact	Reduction
One-Light Print	.111	.202
Timed Uncorrected Print	.1644	.2555
Subsequent Corrected Print (Color and Density)	.111	.202
Black and White Print (From Color Negative)	.0528	.0698

Note: Quality of color negative cannot be determined from black and white print.

INTERPOSITIVES

		Contact	Reduction
From Color Negative (Not Previously Timed by Du Art)	M/C $25.00	.5209	.5659
From Color Negative (Previously Timed and Corrected by Du Art)	M/C $25.00	.3909	.4359
Black and White Pan Master (7253)	M/C $15.00	.1177	.1622
A and B Roll Printing	Add	.045	.065
Additional Roll	Add	.045	.065
Cord to Cord	M/C $20.00 Add	.107	.107
From Color Interpositive (Type 7249)		*	*

INTERNEGATIVES

		Contact	Reduction
From Separation Masters	M/C $25.00	*	.5393
From Interpositives, Reversal Originals or Prints	M/C $15.00	.2260	.2715
From Color Negative (Reversal Stock) (#7249)		*	*
Unsqueezed From 35mm Master	M/C $25.00	——	.3572
Scanning (For Unsqueezed Internegative) Per 1,000 Ft. 35mm Reel	$25.00 per reel		
A and B Roll Printing	Add	.045	.065
Additional Roll	Add	.045	.065
Cord to Cord	Add	.107	.107
From Wide Screen Masters to TV Aspect Ratio	Add	——	.045

RELEASE PRINTS (SUBJECTS OVER 200 FEET IN LENGTH)

	Contact	Reduction
First Trial Answer Print	.1751	.2636
Check Print From Internegative	.111	.202
Single Print Order	.1002	.1323
2—15 Print Order	.0894	.1163
16—30 Print Order	.0787	.1056
31—60 Print Order	.068	.0991
61—100 Print Order	.0658	.0937
A and B Roll Printing .... Add	.0572	.0588
Additional Roll .... Add	.0572	.0588
Cord to Cord ....M/C per roll $15.00 Add	.107	.107
Superimposed Titles .... Add	——	.0155

*Prices on Request

TV SPOTS (ANY LENGTH) AND SMALL ROLLS (UNDER 200 FEET)

	Price Per Foot	
	Contact	Reduction
First Trial Color Composite Answer Print,		
First 50 Feet or Less	$24.25	$64.25
Additional Footage	.3318	1.165
From A and B .... Add	.0572	.0588
Additional Roll .... Add	.0572	.0588

SUBSEQUENT PRINTING

Up to 500 Feet .... Per Negative M/C $16.00	.1498	.2086
501 to 1,000 Feet .... Per Negative	.129	.1716
1,001 to 2,500 Feet .... Per Negative	.1227	.1550
2,501 to 4,000 Feet .... Per Negative	.1071	.1446
4,001 to 6,000 Feet .... Per Negative	.1019	.1394
6,001 to 10,000 Feet .... Per Negative	.0915	.1290
10,001 to 15,000 Feet .... Per Negative	.0801	.1157
15,001 Feet and Over .... Per Negative	.0697	.1027

When laboratory is required to break down timed negative containing more than one TV Spot, there will be no charge for negative labor, but there will be a $7.50 charge per spot for printing set up.

Since most negatives show excessive wear after approximately 100 prints have been made therefrom, we recommend that additional negatives be supplied thereafter.

MISCELLANEOUS

Fades	$2.50 each
Dissolves	$5.00 each

Effects Charged on Answer Prints Only

Short Scene Printing .... Add Per Foot	.006
Unspliced Raw Stock .... Add Per Foot	.01

Thread-Up Waste — Add 3% To Negative Footage — Minimum 8 Feet Per Item

Minimum Charge $11.00 Per Item Except Where Noted

COLOR REVERSAL

EKTACHROME — GEVACHROME — KODACHROME

16MM AND 35MM

16MM DEVELOPING

	Price Per Foot	Minimum
Commercial Ektachrome (ECO)	.0577	$11.00
High Speed Ektachrome (MS and EF)	.0809	11.00
Ektachrome Forced Processing .... Add	.0964	32.25
Color Intermediate (#7249)	*	*
Gevachrome 600 and 605	*	*
Gevachrome Forced Processing .... Add	*	*

35MM DEVELOPING

Commercial Ektachrome (ECO)	*	*
High Speed Ektachrome (MS and EF)	*	*
Forced Processing .... Add	*	*
Color Intermediate (=5249)	*	*

16 MM DAILIES OR RUSHES

	Price Per Foot
One-Light Work Print (Gevachrome 903 or Kodachrome 7387)	.0834
Timed Work Print (Gevachrome 903 or Kodachrome 7387)	.1082
Gevachrome Optical Sound Dailies Add	.1150
One-Light Work Print (Ektachrome 7389)	*
Timed Work Print (Ektachrome 7389)	*
Black and White Reversal (≠7360)	.0658
One-Light Work Print (Ektachrome 7388)	.1234
Timed Work Print (Ektachrome 7388)	.1482

IF SPLICED STOCK REQUESTED ON DAILIES DEDUCT .02 PER FOOT

35mm Color Reversal Dailies or Prints and Masters	*

16MM REVERSAL MASTERS

		Contact	Reduction
One to One Optical Ektachrome (ECO)	M/C $32.25	.56	— —
One to One Low Contrast Gevachrome		*	
Commercial Ektachrome (ECO) (Contact)	M/C $32.25	.2678	.3998
Low Contrast Gevachrome		*	*
A and B Roll	Add	.045	.065
Additional Roll	Add	.045	.065
Cord to Cord	M/C Per Roll $15.00 Add	.107	.107

RELEASE PRINTS (GEVACHROME 903/ KODACHROME 7387 / EKTACHROME 7389 / OVER 200 FEET)

	Contact (Single Strand)	Contact (A & B)	Reduction
First Trial Answer Print	.1323	.1884	.16
Single Print Order	.1216	.1691	.14
2 to 10 Print Order	.1163	.153	.132
11 to 25 Print Order	.1109	.1423	.125
26 Prints and Over	.1063	.1325	.12
Print on Ektachrome Type 7388 (Picture Only) . . . . Add	.0475	.0475	.0475
Small Rolls (Not Including TV Commercial Spots) . . . . M/C $15.00 Add	.02	.02	.02
Cord to Cord . . . . M/C Per Roll $15.00 Add	.107	.107	.107
Printing From Additional Roll (C, D, etc.) . . . . Add	.045	.045	.065
Print on Ektachrome Type 7389 . . . . Add	*	*	

TV COMMERCIAL SPOTS (GEVACHROME 903 / KODACHROME 7387 / EKTACHROME 7389)

	Contact	Reduction
First Trial Answer Print	.44	$ 1.20
Minimum Charge	$48.25	$64.25
A and B Roll . . . . Add	.05	.05
TV Print on Ektachrome Type 7388 (Picture Only) . . . . Add	.0475	.0475
Subsequent Prints . . . . M/C $20.00	.1675	.1785
TV Print on Ektachrome Type 7389 . . . . Add	*	*

When laboratory is required to break down timed preprint material
containing more than one TV Spot, there will be no charge for negative labor,
but there will be a $7.50 charge per spot for printing set up.

MISCELLANEOUS

Fades	$2.50 each
Dissolves	$5.00 each
Zero Cut	$2.50 each

Effects Charged on Answer Prints Only

Short Scenes . . . . Add Per Foot	.01
Unspliced Raw Stock . . . . Add Per Foot	.02
Magnetic to Optical Printing . . . . M/C $25.00 Add Per Foot	.02

Thread-Up Waste — Add 3% to Negative Footage — Minimum 8 Feet Per Item

Minimum Charge $11.00 Per Item Except Where Noted

*Prices On Request.

35MM BLACK AND WHITE

RUSHES OR DAILIES

	Price Per Foot
Develop Picture Negative	.0348
Develop Sound Negative	.0348
Print Picture Only	.0620
Print Sound Only	.0620
Reversal Print From Work Print (#5360)	.0725

MASTERS AND DUPE NEGATIVES

	Master	Dupe Negative
Picture	.0858	.1296
Composite	.0891	.1403
Blow Up From 16mm Single Run to 35mm (Per 35mm Ft.) .... M/C $20.00	.25	.25
Reversal type 5360	.0775	.0775
A and B Roll Printing .... Add	.0536	.0536
Cord to Cord .... M/C Per Roll $7.50 Add	.0321	.0321
Superimposed Titles .... Add	.0095	––

RELEASE PRINTS (REELS OVER 500 FEET)

First Trial Answer Print	.0593
Single Print	.0513
2–10 Prints	.0476
11–25 Prints	.0443
26–50 Prints	.0422
A and B Prints .... Add	.0218
Superimposed Titles .... Add	.0095

TV SPOTS AND SMALL ROLLS (LESS THAN 500 FEET)

First Trial Answer Print	.0740
Up to 2,500 Feet Per Roll	.0620
2,501 to 6,250 Feet Per Roll	.0593
6,251 to 10,000 Feet Per Roll	.0540
10,001 to 25,000 Feet Per Roll	.0508
25,001 Feet and Over Per Roll	.0465
Filmstrips	.07

MISCELLANEOUS

	Price Per Foot
Unspliced Raw Stock Print .... Add Per Foot	.0054
Fades .... Each	$ 3.50
Dissolves .... Each	7.00

Note: Charge for effects will be made on answer print only.

Cord to Cord (Except where noted)	.0321

Note: Nitrate preprint materials require a considerable amount of special handling which necessitates a surcharge of 10% to the above listed prices.

Since nitrate material is of a highly flammable nature, the laboratory will process only ONE subject at a time.

Thread-Up Waste — Add 2% To Negative Footage — Minimum 8 Feet Per Item

Minimum Charge $11.00 Per Item Except Where Noted

16MM BLACK AND WHITE

RUSHES OR DAILIES

	Price Per Foot
Develop Picture Negative	.0348
Develop Sound Negative	.0348

	Contact	Reduction
Print Picture Only	.0556	.0586
Print Sound Only	.0556	.0586
Reversal Print From Work Print (Picture Only) (7360)	.0658	.0700
Reversal Print From Work Print Composite (7360)	.0728	.0778

MASTERS AND DUPE NEGATIVES

	Master		Dupe Negative	
	Contact	Reduction	Contact	Reduction
Picture	.0689	.0743	.1042	.1074
Composite	.0743	.0796	.1096	.1128
Reversal Type 7360	.0681	.0735	.0881	.0935
Picture (Unsqueezed) ....M/C $20.00	—	.1800	—	.2065
Wide Screen To TV Aspect ....M/C $20.00	—	.135	—	.1575
Scanning	$25.00 per roll			
One to One Optical ....M/C $25.00	.3788	—	.3908	—
A and B ....Add	.0375	.0425	.0375	.0425
Cord to Cord ....M/C Per Roll $10.00 Add	.0350	.04	.0350	.04
Superimposed Titles ....Add	—	.016	—	—
Wet Gate Printing ....Add	.0125	—	.0125	—

RELEASE PRINTS (OVER 200 FEET)

	Contact	Reduction
First Trial Answer Print	.0552	.0579
Single Print	.0494	.0509
2–10 Prints	.0418	.0467
11–25 Prints	.0397	.0456
26–50 Prints	.0360	.0450
Over 50 Prints	.0343	.0445
A and B Release Printing ....Add Per Foot	.0218	.025
Additional Roll ....Add	.0218	.025
Cord to Cord ....M/C Per Roll $7.50 Add	.0321	.0321
Superimposed Titles ....Add	.0075	.0075
Wet Gate Printing ....Add	.0125	—

TV SPOTS AND ROLLS LESS THAN 200 FEET

	Price Per Foot	
	Contact	Reduction
First Trial Answer Print	.0669	.0689
Up to 1,000 Feet Per Roll	.0569	.0589
1,001 to 2,500 Feet Per Roll	.0552	.0557
2,501 to 5,000 Feet Per Roll	.0504	.0525
5,001 to 10,000 Feet Per Roll	.0472	.0494
10,001 Feet and Over	.0397	.0472
A and B Printing ....Add Per Foot	.0214	.0268
Additional Roll ....Add	.0214	.0268

Since most negatives show excessive wear after approximately 100 prints have been made therefrom, we recommend that additional negatives be supplied thereafter.

MISCELLANEOUS

Fades	$ 2.14 each
Dissolves	$ 4.28 each
Short Scene Printing ....Add	.0075
Unspliced Raw Stock Print ....Add Per Foot	.0054
Low Contrast Flashing of Prints (K Process) ....Add	.015

A charge for effects will be made on answer print only

Thread-Up Waste — Add 2% To Negative Footage — Minimum 8 Feet Per Item

Minimum Charge $7.50 Per Item Except Where Noted

16MM BLACK AND WHITE REVERSAL
LEADERS — CODING — SLITTING — ULTRA SONIC CLEANING

		Price Per Foot 16MM	Price Per Foot 16MM
Reversal Developing	Minimum Charge	$7.50	.0448

REVERSAL PRINTING

		Contact	Reduction
Reversal Type (7360)		.0658	.0708
One-Light Print (Type 7361)		.094	.099
Timed Print Picture (Type 7361)		.1021	.1071
One-Light Print (Panchromatic Stock)		.1071	.1121
Timed Print Picture (Panchromatic Stock)		.1171	.1221
With Sound	Add	.0049	.0049
A and B Printing	Add	.0249	.0249
Cord to Cord .... M/C per roll $7.50	Add	.0259	.0259
Unspliced Raw Stock	Add	.01	.01
Fades or Zero Cut	Each	$ 2.14	$ 2.14
Dissolves	Each	$ 4.28	$ 4.28
Short Scene Printing	Add	.0075	.0075
Minimum Charge		$7.50 per item	

		Price Per Foot 16MM	Price Per Foot 35MM
LEADERS			
White Leader	M/C $5.00	.0109	.02
Black Leader	M/C $5.00	.0268	.0326
Clear Leader	M/C $5.00	.02	.0265
Academy Leader (Negative Stock)	M/C $5.00	.0999	.1114
Academy Leader (Positive Stock)	M/C $5.00	.0429	.0518
Academy Leader (Positive Stock Develop Low Contrast)	M/C $5.00	.0679	.0768
Coding (Edge Numbering)		.01	.01
Minimum Charge		$ 7.50	$ 7.50
Ultra Sonic Cleaning of Print		.01	.01
Minimum Charge		$ 7.50	$ 7.50

Thread-Up Waste — Add 2% to Negative Footage — Minimum 8 Feet Per Item

ADDITIONAL LABORATORY SERVICES

LABOR

Negative Matching	*
Cording Off Negative	$9.00 per hour
Lining Up (Synchronizing) Picture & Track Negative	$12.00 per hour
Lining Up (Synchronizing) Picture & Magnetic Sound Tape	$12.00 per hour
Splicing Negative	$9.00 per hour
Selecting Takes	$9.00 per hour
Splicing Positive	$8.00 per hour
Mounting on Reels	$ .25 per reel
Assembling on Core	$ .25 per reel
Inspection by Projection of Preprint Material and Letter Reports	$10.00 per reel
Examination and Identifying Preprint Material	$9.00 per hour
Overtime Labor	$16.50 per man hr.
Overtime Labor — Sunday and Beyond 8 hours Saturday	$25.00 per man hr.

There will be an additional plant opening charge added to labor charges for opening on Saturday, Sunday, or Union Holidays.

Prices furnished upon request.

8MM EASTMAN COLOR OR BLACK AND WHITE POSITIVE

The laboratory offers services for processing of Standard and Super 8mm film — both optical and magnetic sound.

Prices furnished upon request.

Film Treatment	*

TITLE CARD PHOTOGRAPHING

Main Titles or Sub Titles	*

*Prices On Request

TERMS AND CONDITIONS

1. Du Art Film Laboratories, Inc. and Du Art Color Corporation and/or their subsidiary and affiliated Corporations ("Du Art") shall not be liable to Customer or others for loss or damage of any kind whatsoever due to delays or failure in performance caused directly or indirectly by acts of God, strikes or other labor stoppages, fire, failure of transportation agencies or public utilities, the elements, war, shortages of labor or material, government regulation, damage or accident to or failure to machinery or equipment, injury or damage to, or loss of, film and other property delivered to Du Art, or due to any other cause whether or not similar to any of the foregoing causes and whether or not the injury, loss or damage occurs while in Du Art's custody or while in transit.

2. Du Art will not insure any of Customer's film and other property while in the possession of Du Art or while in transit and all such film and other property delivered to Du Art are accepted upon the express understanding and condition that they are fully insured by Customer against all loss or damage from any cause whatsoever, including negligence, whether suffered while in Du Art's possession or control, or otherwise, and the Customer waives all rights of subrogation; and the Customer agrees that such insurance does not and will not give the insurer any recourse or rights of subrogation against Du Art. Notwithstanding the foregoing, in the event of loss, damage or destruction of any such film and other property as a result of Du Art's negligence, Du Art will voluntarily, without admission of liability or responsibility, reimburse Customer for the cost of the raw stock. Any claim for such reimbursement must be made by written notice to Du Art within 30 days after delivery of such film and other property to Customer or its designee or notice of its loss or damage, whichever is the sooner, and unless suit is instituted within 1 year thereafter. All film and other property delivered to Du Art may be moved to or kept at such place or places as Du Art may deem desirable, there being no promise or representation, express or implied, that such film and other property delivered for any purpose will be retained or kept at its premises or at any other designated place.

3. If the work requested by Customer requires the film or other property to be delivered to a third party for performance of services in connection therewith, Customer authorizes Du Art to deliver such film and other property to such third party but Du Art shall have no liability for any loss or damage resulting from the negligence of such third party or occurring while the film or other property is in transit to and from such third party.

4. All prices are F.O.B. Du Art's Laboratory. Unless written instructions are received, Du Art will ship all film and other property by such method of transportation as Du Art deems advisable, with shipping expenses payable by Customer.

5. Prices are subject to change, due to any fluctuation in the cost of raw stock, material or taxes thereon, and/or union labor costs, retroactive to the effective date thereof. All prices are subject to any applicable federal, state or local excise, sales or use taxes.

6. Du Art shall be entitled to charge for overtime labor as instructed by Customer and for work performed on Saturdays, Sundays and legal holidays at the request of Customer, which by virtue of any labor contracts Du Art has entered into or may enter into with a Union, Du Art shall be required to pay overtime rates for such labor.

7. Du Art may require any Customer to retake possession of any and all film and other property held for Customer. If such film and other property has been inactive for more than 6 months, then Du Art may, after 30 days written notice, either send the same to a public warehouse in the name of the Customer or may destroy said film and other property or may charge the Customer for storing the same at the rate established by Du Art from time to time. All such charges are to be secured by Customer's rights in and to such film and other property.

8. All invoices issued by Du Art are payable NET 30 days. Interest at legal rates will be charged on all invoices not paid when due, and if placed for collection, Customer agrees to pay all costs of collection, including reasonable attorney's fees not to exceed 20% of amount owed. Any and all charges shall be secured by all property held for

Customer and whether or not as herefrom ... Du Art with respect to such property, including, but not limited to copyrights, patents and trademarks whether issued under the laws of the United States or otherwise.

9. If a print made by Du Art is found to be defective, or shipped or labeled in error, Du Art's sole liability will be promptly to replace or repair such defective print and/or correct such error in shipment at its expense, provided written notice of such imperfection or such error in labeling or shipment is given to Du Art within 10 days after its arrival at destination. Customer shall return such print to Du Art if it shall so request. In no event, including negligence, shall Du Art be liable for any consequential damages.

10. Prices shown in this list are for materials and services deemed by Du Art to require standard laboratory processing and handling. Old, shrunken or damaged negatives or pre-print materials, or those which are not in a normal or usual photographical or physical condition are accepted for printing and laboratory work, service and labor with the understanding that a charge will be made for the additional time and/or materials which are required to comply with any orders submitted, but in no event will Du Art guarantee satisfactory results from such negatives or pre-print materials. Since color film dyes may change in time, reorders for prints from old color negatives may yield unsatisfactory color balance requiring a new answer print. Du Art will attempt at all times to notify Customer before entering orders requiring additional charges. When special requirements, with increased cost to the Customer, are encountered after an order is placed in process, the Customer will be notified immediately of the additional charges.

11. The Customer assumes all liability under the copyright laws and under any other laws, both federal and state, arising out of the fulfillments by Du Art of any services for the account of the Customer, who agrees to indemnify and hold Du Art free and harmless of any and all suits, claims, damages, liabilities and expenses (including attorneys' fees) which may arise directly or indirectly from the performance of such services by Du Art for the Customer.

12. The exercise by Du Art of any right or remedy hereunder shall not preclude its right to enforce any one or more other remedies. Nothing contained herein shall be deemed to limit or prejudice the rights of Du Art under the Lien Law of the State of New York or any other state or territory in which Laboratory renders services, manufactures prints and furnishes materials. Customer agrees that if Laboratory shall enforce its rights under any Lien Law, it or any other party acquiring title to any film at public or private sale shall have and is hereby granted an unrestricted license to distribute, exhibit and otherwise exploit such film by all media for its own account.

13. Any increase in a previous order must be on a new purchase order form. When Customer reduces an order, the instructions must be in writing. All services and/or materials already performed or manufactured at the time of receipt of such reduction will be chargeable to Customer. Reductions necessarily cause delays in completion of orders. Upon cancellation of an order, Customer agrees to pay Du Art its charges for services and materials furnished up until the time of receipt of such cancellation.

14. Du Art will endeavor to keep its Customers advised concerning the exposure, photographic quality and physical condition of the negative films received from them for processing but it shall not be responsible for failure to do so.

15. Customer acknowledges that all sales and contracts for sale are made in the State of New York. All actions against Customer may be brought in the State of New York, and Customer expressly consents to the jurisdiction of the Courts of the State of New York.

16. No waiver, alteration or modification of the terms and conditions hereof shall be binding unless in writing and signed by a corporate officer of Du Art. Du Art has made no representations, warranties or agreements, express or implied, except as specifically set forth in these "Terms and Conditions."

Chapter 6

Sound Costs

Sound is one of the most difficult production costs to estimate with limited production experience. Although there are some very broad rules to follow, each production will vary according to its particular needs. For example, a narration by a well known star could make your budget higher than a narration by a talented but unknown actor, because of his fee. Or, original music performed by a group of eight has to raise the cost of your production more than if you used "canned" music or music in the Public Domain. These are the variables that can change your budget drastically.

Sound is a cost factor in three major areas of your production. The first time you are involved with processing and developing sound is when production begins and the sound that has been recorded must be transferred. The second time involvement with sound arises is during editing when sound effects and-or music and-or narration are recorded. The third and final time is during the mix. To give continuity to your sound and keep the areas of responsibility to a minimum, it is advisable to do all sound work—transfers, music and effects, recording, and mixing—at the same facility.

RECORDING

During film production, sound is usually recorded on ¼-inch audio tape because of the high quality and the portability of the recording equipment. It is also much cheaper than recording on 16mm or 35mm magnetic film. After filming has been completed, the sound is transferred from the tape to 16mm or 35mm magnetic film to be compatible with the picture for editing purposes.

During video tape production, the sound is recorded on the same magnetic tape as the picture and need not be removed or transferred at all. It is handled simultaneously during editing, whereas on film the sound is separate. (The only exception to this in film is a case of low-budget news or documentary filming where sound is recorded simultaneously, either magnetically or optically, on the same film and with the same camera as the picture. Since the sound does not parallel the corresponding picture but, instead, is a number of frames ahead, editing becomes very difficult and impractical.)

TRANSFERS

When estimating transfer charges, include the costs for transfer time in your budget, plus the 16mm or 35mm magnetic film. The transfer costs are broken into two categories: time (labor) and material (stock). Labor is usually charged on an hourly basis and material on a per foot basis.

If the transfer is ordered "flat," that is, with no electronic equalization of the sound quality, the estimated transfer time should be approximately 1½ times the running time of the tapes. This allows time for the transfer studio to set up and change reels. Therefore, if you have two hours of ¼-inch tape that needs to be transferred to magnetic track, you would budget three hours of time at the applicable hourly rate. In addition, you would budget the amount of magnetic stock to be used on a footage basis. Audio tape is usually recorded at 7½ ips (inches per second). Estimates for magnetic track are based on film footages for a 10-minute reel: 400 feet in 16mm and 1000 feet in 35mm. Two hours of 16 magnetic track equals 4,800 feet of 16 magnetic track and two hours of 35 magnetic track equals 12,000 feet of 35 magnetic track.

However, if the transfer man is asked to listen to all the recorded material and equalize it, the labor charges will increase according to the utilization of his time. Although it is not necessary to equalize sound when it is transferred, some producers and directors prefer it. This way the editor can hear the sound at its best and any marginal sound problems can be resolved before the mix. For films with a large amount of sound daily material, such as features and documentaries, the extra cost for corrected transfers is not warranted.

The rates for transferring sound depend on who is doing it. Many laboratories offer free sound transfers as a way of inducing you to let the lab process dailies. In instances such as these, only the time is free; you pay for the 16mm or 35mm magnetic stock. Others, whose rates may be higher, are sound studios who are specialists in sound. Again, the desired end product will help determine your choice of facility.

The charges for transfers, then, are based on time and material. Estimate time at 1½ to two times the running length of the material to be transferred. Sound should be transferred on a daily basis rather than waiting until the end of the production. Although this costs a little more, the extra expense is worth it if such problems as excessive camera noise, out-of-sync equipment, defective equipment, etc., are detected. By finding this out early in production, you can take the necessary steps to correct it immediately rather than finding out after the production is over, when it might be too late or too expensive to do anything about it. Once the sound has been transferred, the editor or his assistant will put it into synchronization with the dailies (match the picture and track).

After the sound transfers have been made and the track put into sync with the picture, there are no more additional sound charges until it is time to incorporate music and-or sound effects into the production, record narration, and to mix the production.

MUSIC

When choosing music, there are two general types available: 1) "canned" or stock, and 2) original. Under the category of "canned" music, there are three types—copyrighted music, that in the Public Domain, and that available through music libraries. Usually, existing recorded music is cheaper than original music.

If you use stock music that still retains the composer's copyright, two licenses must be obtained. The first is from the publisher who owns the copyright and the second from the record company that issued the recording. The fees for these licenses depend on the type of production, where it will be seen, and how often it will run. Sometimes a third payment is required if a vocal or instrumental artist is featured on the record. This licensing procedure applies to both popular and classical records. Usually, the two fees are in the same amount. The charges can range from $100 for each license up to $5,000, depending on the music you have selected. Often you are limited to the number of times you may run your production and where you may run it before additional monies must be paid to the publisher, record company, and, where applicable, the artist.

A variation on this is your own arrangement of a well known standard or popular song. Again, permission must be received from the publisher and record company, and the license must stipulate instrumental and-or vocal use. It will list the geographical areas of use, and it will limit the number of years the license will be in effect. When this arrangement is recorded, the same payments and conditions are required as if it were original music.

Another source of canned music is that in the Public Domain. This is music whose copyrights have expired. There is no charge for this music. A word of caution, though. If the version you are using is a new arrangement, has the addition of lyrics, or is somehow different from the original version, permission must be received from the owner, similar to the clearance required for copyrighted music, and licensing fees paid.

A third source of canned music is that available through music libraries. There is a wide variety including everything from "hot rock" to heavy classics. Payment to the music library is made only once and the music may be used indefinitely. The only time an additional payment is required is if the same music is used in a revision or new version of your production. The prices range from $25 to $500, depending on the length of your production and how much work must be done by the music library. If you want the sound of original music for the price of library music, the editor at the library can "score" your production from existing music. Although there is a charge for this, it is still cheaper than original music.

How much does original music cost? Minimum $1,000 and up. Original music is expensive because you must pay a composing and arranging fee, studio time, union scale to the performers (both musicians and, if used, singers), pension and welfare contributions for the performers, cartage (fees paid to the musicians for carrying their own instruments), and the necessary payroll taxes. In addition to paying for the original recording, residuals must be paid to all performing talent for every 13-week cycle it is used. Check with the local American Federation of Musicians (AFM) and American Federation of Television and Radio Artists (AFTRA) offices for the talent rates applicable to your area.

Your choice of music, then, is influenced two ways. First, by the type of production and, second, by the restrictions of your budget. If there are no limits to the amount of money that can be spent, use original music. Otherwise, you are restricted to music that has already been recorded.

SOUND EFFECTS

Another item to be included in your budget is sound effects. Again, as with music, there is a wide range in prices. If the necessary sound effects are not obtainable during actual production, there are several ways of incorporating them into your production. The cheapest method is to buy a record of the most often used effects. This is good if the effects needed are fairly common. The cost of the record can be as low as $5.

For a more unusual effect, purchase effects from a sound effects library. Quality and prices of the effects will vary greatly, depending on the type of effect and where it is being purchased. Often a music library can also provide sound effects.

A third method is to have the effects custom made. Although this can be quite expensive, it might be the only solution for the needs of your production. These can cost up to $50 an effect; however, you are assured of the right effect and won't have to compromise with a standard effect.

If a number of sound effects are needed, it might be cheaper to hire a good sound man for the day, rent the necessary recording equipment, and have him get the specific effects needed. This is practical only when 10 or more effects are needed and if the effects are easily obtainable in one day. If more than one day is needed to record these effects, the costs become prohibitive and it is cheaper to use existing effects or have them custom made.

NARRATION

At the same time music and effects tracks are being made, the narration recording can be done. A narration recording or voice-over is easy to budget. Your talent charges are included in the "talent" section of your budget. The only other expense item is the charge for studio time. For a commercial, budget a minimum of one-half hour; for a half-hour show, 2 hours; for an hour show, four hours. The exact amount of time you should budget will depend on the complexity of your production.

MIXING

The mix is the next step in the area of sound. What is a mix? Where does it occur in the production process? This is the point where all sound is brought together, balanced and equalized, and combined onto one composite sound track. How do you estimate the costs? Since there are so many variables, it is difficult to come up with a standard formula. However, if you understand the full mixing process, you will be able to estimate more precisely the time and costs for a mix. In video tape, mixing is usually part of the editing process (see Chapter 12).

In film, after the basic picture editing has been completed, the sound tracks—music, sound effects and narration—are edited in sync with the picture. The editor then makes cue sheets that tell the sound mixer where each sound track comes in and goes out. Since the cue sheets are the guide to the mixer, they must be prepared carefully. Too many times this important final step is turned over to an assistant editor because the editor's energy and enthusiasm have waned over the long weeks of editing. Don't let this happen or the mix will suffer.

The time needed for a mix depends on many variables— the length of the production, the number of sound tracks, the complexity of the tracks, the amount of track equalization required, and the number of people present at the mix. Sometimes a premix is budgeted. This can save you time and money in the actual mix, since the mixer has an opportunity to hear all the tracks, set his levels, and possibly detect flaws in the tracks.

To determine the exact amount of time to budget, study your script or storyboard closely. A 30-second commercial with music and narration could take only five minutes. However, if the sound needs to be corrected or sound effects incorporated or other changes made, this same commercial could take as much as two hours.

Mixing time is booked in half-hour increments and is charged on an hourly basis. Usually, you book the amount of time you think it will take you to mix your production and the sound studio will add a half hour as bumper between you and the next client. Obviously, this bumper time is not included when you book the whole day. You can use the bumper if you need it; however, if you don't use it, you will not be billed for it. When estimating your production, include the cost for this half hour in your budget. It's better to over-estimate than to under-estimate. The hourly price quoted by the sound house covers the cost of the studio, the mixer, plus the labor involved in transferring the final mix to the medium requested; i.e., magnetic or optical track. Most sound houses give you one free transfer with your mix. That is, they will take your ¼-inch audio tape mix and transfer it to 16mm or 35mm magnetic track, or go directly to an optical negative.

It is advisable to use the same sound studio and mixer for all work pertaining to any one production. It gives continuity to the sound and reduces the chances for error by keeping all the sound responsibility in one location.

In summary, mixing charges are based on time and material. The studio charges are billed on an hourly basis, ¼-

inch tape on a per roll basis, and the 16mm and 35mm magnetic track on a per foot basis. Watch for hidden charges such as setup time, minimum reels, delivery, copy tapes, etc. (Fig. 6-1). Although there is no set formula for determining mixing time, take into consideration the length of your production, the number of sound effects, the music, the voice

studios

	MON.-FRI. 8:30 am-5 pm	MON.-FRI. 5 PM-12 M SATURDAY 8:30 am-5 pm	SUNDAY SAT. after 5 PM MON.-FRI. 12 M-8:30 AM
Studio "A"			
Narration:	$30.00	$40.00	$50.00
Music Recording:	$40.00	$50.00	$60.00
Studio "B"			
Narration:	$20.00	$30.00	$40.00
Music Recording:	$30.00	$40.00	$50.00
Studio "C"			
Narration:	$20.00	$30.00	$40.00

Stereo or Mono—One, Two, Four, or Eight Track
Studio set-up for music $10.00
Additional Engineer when required $10.00/hr.
(Eve., Sat. and Sun. $15.00)
Scheduled time will be charged unless cancelled 24 hours in advance.

recording tape

Studio-Master Grade

1200'—¼"	$ 5.00	2400'—¼"	$10.00
1200'—½"	10.00	2400'—½"	20.00
1200'—1"	20.00	2400'—1"	40.00

programming, editing & post mixing

	MON.-FRI. 8:30 AM-5 PM	MON.-FRI. 5 PM-12 M SAT. to 5 PM
Monaural & Single Track	$20.00	$30.00
Stereo, 2, 4 & 8 Track	25.00	35.00

Prices are minimum of ½ hour, plus ¼ hour increments.

Add $15.00 per hour to above rates for Saturday 8 AM to 5 PM—Monday-Friday 5 PM to 12 M.

Add $25.00 per hour to above rates for Sunday, Holidays, Saturday after 5 PM, Monday-Friday after 12 M.

film recording services

	MON.-FRI. 8 AM-5 PM per hour
Live Recording—To Picture	
Studio "B" ¼" Sync Tape	$30.00
(non-instrumental)	
Studio "A" ¼" Sync Tape	50.00
(music or narration)	
Film Department Narration Studio	45.00
¼" Sync Tape, 16mm or 35mm magnetic film (narration only)	
Wild Live Recording—No Projection	
Studio "B" ¼" Sync Tape	20.00
(non-instrumental)	
Studio "A" ¼" Sync Tape	40.00
(music or narration)	
Film Department Narration Studio	35.00
¼" Sync Tape, 16mm or 35mm magnetic film (narration only)	
Transfers	
Rerecording from one source to or from any medium	35.00
¼" Sync Tape, 16mm or 35mm magnetic film—exact copying	
Mixing—Projection—Interlock	
For transfer or mixing	45.00
Where equalizing, balancing tracks, level changes, mixing thru 6 channel console is required	
Screening—Viewing Theater	
Composite Picture	25.00
35mm or 16mm	
Interlock Picture with one magnetic track	30.00
35mm or 16mm	
Interlock Picture with 2 to 5 magnetic tracks	45.00
35mm or 16mm	
Film Editing	
Facilities and one engineer	20.00
Film Stock—Minimum 250 ft.	
16mm magnetic	.025 per ft.
35mm magnetic	.03 per ft.
Complete Sound Effects and Music Libraries Available for All Film Recording	

Prices are per hour, charged at quarter hour increments

Fig. 6-1. Sample sound service rate card.

and-or narration tracks, to help you determine the length of the mix. Never budget less than one hour. For a commercial, figure 1½ hours; for a half-hour documentary, three hours; for an hour show, eight hours; and a feature film, three days. These are just basic times; the actual time estimate will depend on the sound elements of your particular production.

If you are in doubt when estimating the sound elements in your production, call the sound house you will be using and ask their advice. The advice is free and they are glad to give it, since it makes their job easier. You won't have under- or over-estimated in the area of sound and there will be fewer problems during production. Also, by seeking their advice or merely getting an affirmation of your figures, your estimate will be more precise and accurate.

Chapter 7
Production Personnel

In any production, film or video tape, there are two general categories of personnel: technical and creative. "Technical" refers to those people who primarily operate equipment and who are involved in a production only during the actual physical production itself. This includes cameramen, soundmen, grips, gaffers, etc. "Creative," on the other hand, refers to those people who have been responsible for getting the idea, planning it, and then executing it. This includes producers, directors, and production managers, as well as, peripherally, make-up artists, wardrobe handlers, and hairdressers. This is not to imply that technicians are not creative. Nor does it mean that a creative person cannot be a technician. For example, there are a number of men, and women, who are combination directors-cameramen. However, for the purpose of this writing it is necessary to establish some delineation and this seems the most logical. The budget form shown in Fig. 7-1 is a guide to estimating the cost of production personnel. As you gain experience, you may wish to make some alterations, but this is a good beginning.

TECHNICAL PERSONNEL

Let's deal with the technical people first. There are four unions that provide technical personnel:

1. National Association of Broadcast Employees and Technicians (NABET).
2. International Alliance of Theatrical and Stage Employees (IATSE).
3. International Brotherhood of Electrical Workers (IBEW).
4. International Brotherhood of Teamsters and Chauffeurs (Teamsters).

NABET is a vertical union; that is, all people are available through the same local. IATSE is a horizontal union;

that is, each category of personnel is under the jurisdiction of IATSE but each has a different local. For example, in New York, film cameramen are IA Local No. 644, film stagehands IA Local No. 52, tape stagehands IA Local No. 1, etc. The only separation in NABET is that there is one local for film and one for video tape. Otherwise, cameramen, stagehands, make-up artists, etc., are all in the same local.

How many technical people must be included in your production? If you are shooting in video tape with one camera and one video tape recorder (VTR), synchronized sound, union, studio, the minimum technical crew would be as follows:

    1 Technical director (TD)
    1 Audio man
    1 Video man

```
          PRODUCTION PERSONNEL ( _____ weeks)

$ _____   1.  Producer
  _____   2.  Director
  _____   3.  Director of Photo graphy
  _____   4.  First cameraman
  _____   5.  Second cameraman
  _____   6.  First assistant cameraman ( ___ )
  _____   7.  Second assistant cameraman ( ___ )
  _____   8.  _____
  _____   9.  _____
  _____  10.  Soundman ( , ___ )
  _____  11.  Assistant soundman ( ___ )
  _____  12.  Mixer/Recordist ( ___ )
  _____  13.  _____
  _____  14.  _____
  _____  15.  Production Assistant
  _____  16.  Grip ( ___ )
  _____  17.  Electrician ( ___ )
  _____  18.  Gaffer ( ___ )
  _____  19.  Prop ( ___ )
  _____  20.  _____
  _____  21.  Lighting Director
  _____  22.  Production Manager/Unit Manager
  _____  23.  Script Supervisor
  _____  24.  Make-up Artist ( ___ )
  _____  25.  Hairdresser ( ___ )
  _____  26.  Wardrobe Attendant ( ___ )
  _____  27.  _____
  _____  28.  Pension and Welfare
  _____  29.  Payroll taxes
  _____  30.  Miscellaneous
```

Fig. 7-1. Personnel budget form.

1 Tape man
1 Cameraman
1 Stagehand
1 Lighting director (LD).

Of course, as additional equipment is added so must you add crew members. For the purposes of estimating and budgeting, it is not necessary to discuss, in depth, individual job descriptions and responsibilities. It is only important to be aware of their basic responsibilities.

The technical director (TD) controls the switcher panel and is responsible for all screen effects—fades, dissolves, mattes, etc.—as well as switching camera shots in multiple camera productions. The director determines which shots are to be used; the TD physically executes them for taping. The video man controls the quality of the picture being taped. He balances the color, stabilizes the picture, and rides video level during the entire taping session to be sure it is of maximum quality. The tape man controls the camera(s) electronically and is responsible for the actual physical taping of the production. The balance of the basic crew functions are self-explanatory.

In film, under approximately the same conditions, i.e., one camera, sync sound, studio, union, the minimum technical crew would be as follows:

1 First cameraman (or director of photography)
1 Assistant cameraman
1 Sound man
1 Assistant soundman
1 Grip
1 Prop
1 Gaffer (electrician).

The assistant cameraman and assistant soundman do just what their titles suggest—assist with filming or taking sound by loading and changing the film magazines, loading the audio tape onto the tape recorder, holding the microphone, setting up the camera tripod, etc. In some productions an operative cameraman is optional. The director of photography (D-O-P), or first cameraman, operates the camera (sometimes) and is responsible for the lighting. Even if he doesn't operate the camera, he is responsible for judging the feasibility and probability of the shots called by the director. If it can be done, he either gets the shot as directed or directs the camera operator on how to achieve it, including determining the lenses to be used, filters, etc. Grips, gaffers, and prop men are the film counterparts to video tape stagehands.

Because the rates vary from location to location, it is advisable to contact the business agents of the local unions you are using in your production to get up-to-date listings of all rates. Also get a copy of the contracts explaining the working conditions for the members. In addition to giving you hourly, daily, and weekly rates, the contract should spell out the following:

1. Working hours
2. Overtime
3. Location-studio pay
4. Short turnaround
5. Night differential
6. Golden time
7. Saturday-Sunday work
8. Legal holidays
9. Meal penalties
10. Travel time (see Chapter 10).
11. Per diem (see Chapter 10).
12. Mileage (see Chapter 10).

Does the union have set starting times? For example, there are some unions that require your production to start between the hours of 7 and 10 AM, Monday through Friday. If you start before 7 AM, it is considered overtime; if you run over eight hours, it is considered overtime; and if you run past 6 PM, it is considered overtime, even if your crew has not worked a full 8-hour day.

How many hours constitute a work day? Is it 7, 7½ or 8 hours plus a lunch hour, or 7, 7½ or 8 with a lunch hour? Is there a minimum working day? With some unions, the minimum call is four hours. However, after four hours the unions vary. Some jump from four to eight hours and then pay in hourly increments; others go in hourly increments after the 4-hour minimum. Make sure this information is correct when preparing your budget. If all your crew is from one union, it is not difficult to figure out your technical personnel costs. However, if your crew is represented by a combination of unions, it is not as simple. For example, if your video tape camera crew is NABET and your stage crew is IATSE, there will automatically be some overtime built into your estimate because of the varying hours that constitute a work day and designated starting times. (A note of caution here. Do **not**, under any circumstances, combine unions without first checking with the local business agents as to their compatibility. Some unions are adamant about working with a competitive union.)

How many days are in-studio shooting and how many days on location? Some unions pay straight time-and-a-half for all location work. How many hours rest must your crew have between calls? If the time off between work periods is less than that listed by the union, additional costs for short turnaround will be incurred. The amount to be paid and the number of hours between shifts varies from union to union. Also, if sufficient time is not given between shifts, the production is required to supply food and lodging for the crew. These costs should be included in your budget. With proper scheduling of personnel, short turnaround can usually be kept to a minimum or avoided.

If your script or storyboard needs are such that you must shoot at night, your crew must be paid a night differential. The amount to be paid is determined by the number of hours worked and what the specific hours are. Depending upon what union is used, this can range from 10 to 25 percent over and above the straight time rate of pay. Another term for night differential is "in lieu of" and, instead of a percentage, it is time-and-a-half after a specified hour (usually midnight).

When your crew works ten days straight without a day off, they are on golden time. This amount is double time and they are paid this amount until they get a day off. As you can imagine, it is cheaper to give them at least one day off a week and extend your production for a longer period of time than it is to work your crew straight through and pay such high overtime expenses. The only time golden time might be unavoidable is during, for example, a long sports event such as the Olympics that cannot be re-staged. Even then your crews could be rotated to avoid this expense.

In some unions, work on a Saturday or Sunday is double time, even if those are the only days worked by the crew. Other unions give Saturday and Sunday the same weighting as Monday through Friday. NABET, for example, does not consider Saturday and Sunday overtime days unless your production is into its sixth, or more, straight day of production. If you anticipate much weekend work, make sure you are not restricting yourself, money-wise, by using the unions that will end up costing you the most money.

Each union has a different set of recognized legal holidays. After the three basic ones (accepted by all unions) of Thanksgiving, Christmas, and New Year's, each union varies. The other seven holidays that are to be considered are Lincoln's Birthday, Washington's Birthday, Memorial Day, Independence Day, Labor Day, Columbus' Birthday, and Armistice Day. If the members of the union(s) you are using are asked to work on any of these holidays, they are either paid time-and-a-half or double time, depending upon the specific union involved. Check the rulings closely with your local business agent—it will save you money.

If you plan on working your crew long hours without a break, meal penalties will be incurred. These figures vary from union to union, as well as the number of hours between meal periods and how the amounts are computed. While one union gives a flat amount for a meal penalty, another adds additional money to the hourly pay until a meal break is given.

In addition to these major areas, there are some minor budget areas that should be noted, too.

1. Is the working situation hazardous? Is hazard pay involved?

2. Are you doing government work? How does this affect your budget?

3. How do you budget standby time?

4. What is the latest time you can cancel a crew without incurring a penalty?

5. Is there a weather contingency?

6. Is there going to be a still photographer on the set? How does this affect the cost of the production?

7. How does a change in work schedule affect your budget?

8. Are there any planned on-camera appearances for any of your crew?

9. Does the union work along departmental or non-departmental lines?

10. Does the union allow deferred payments?

11. Are split shifts allowed?

12. Does the job require special clothing, i.e. underwater gear, protective gear, etc.? (See Chapter 15.)

13. Must you provide comfort station facilities? (See Chapter 10.)

14. Does the union require insurance (flight and-or life) on all crew members?

Although these are minor items, they could be costly if overlooked.

Each of the four unions supplying "technical" personnel—NABET, IATSE, IBEW, and the teamsters is governed by some or all of the aforementioned. How do the teamsters fit into the production business? They drive the equipment trucks, haul the generators, and, in short, drive any trucks involved in the production. Their starting times are very rigid and anything other than the authorized 8-hour day becomes overtime. They are also required to stay with the trucks throughout the production. This can be costly if you plan on being on location for any period of time. A teamster is also involved if there is an automobile to be driven on or off the set. For example, in a commercial where a car must be driven onto the set for filming or taping, you would include two teamsters in your budget: one to drive it onto the set and one to drive it off. This is just one example of how an ignorance of the specific union's rulings can cost your production excessive amounts.

CREATIVE PERSONNEL

The unions that provide creative production personnel are, again, NABET and IATSE, plus the Director's Guild of America (DGA). How many creative people must be included in your production? Using the same video tape production we set up for technical personnel with one camera and one VTR, sync sound, studio, union, the minimum creative crew would be as follows:

1 Director
1 Associate director
1 Make-up artist

This is just the minimum. In addition to these basic three, any or all of the following could be needed:

Stage manager
Hairdresser
Wardrobe attendant
Script supervisor
Production assistant

The associate director in a tape production often handles the timing function of the script supervisor. However, if there is a great amount of editing, a script supervisor is a must for continuity of action. A stage manager is needed if two or more cameras are used or there are a number of people in your cast. A wardrobe attendant is needed when clothing or costumes need ironing or altering. Wardrobe is not to be confused with a stylist or costume designer (see Chapter 9). A production assistant (PA), sometimes called a "go-fer," handles the many details not assigned to anyone else. This covers everything from getting coffee for the client, to writing up cue cards, to replacing a broken iron, to ordering lunch. The name comes from asking them to "go for" this or "go for" that; hence, "go-fers." The PA does the many little things that make your production run smoothly. The rest of the categories are self-explanatory.

The minimum film creative crew on a single camera, sync sound, studio, union production would be:

1 Director
1 Assistant director
1 Script supervisor

In addition to these basic three, any or all of the following could be needed:

Production (or unit) manager
Hairdresser
Wardrobe attendant
Make-up artist
Production assistant

It is advisable to have a production manager in your crew. He is responsible for the control of the production and keeps a close check on monies spent. As much as possible he attempts to keep the actual budget in line with the original estimate. He issues crew calls, establishes the production schedule, orders equipment, etc. In short, he coordinates the production to suit the needs and desires of the producer and director.

In most union productions, a production manager is required. However, if you are working nonunion or on a limited budget, this could be handled several ways. You could hire a nonunion but experienced production manager; you could hire a company's service that specializes in this function; or, you could handle the job yourself as a combination producer-production manager (only as a last resort). A good production manager is an asset to any production, because whatever money is expended for his services is easily saved by his experienced handling of the budget and the production. The same IATSE and NABET contract conditions discussed earlier for technical people apply to the creative people also.

The same questions and cost areas apply to the DGA, too, with one exception. Rather than dealing with various local business agents, there are only two locals to be considered—the west coast and the east coast—each with a film category and a tape category. For example, if you have signed an east coast agreement with the DGA, no matter where your production is being shot or where your production office is, the east coast rates will apply. Conversely, the west coast rates apply if you have signed a west coast agreement.

The category of producer is not as easily defined as the others. There are as many definitions for the role of producer as there are producers. For the purposes of estimating, let's assume the producer is the originator of the concept, has arranged for the financing, and is the final decision maker on the production. How much should be included for a producer in your estimate? Since there is no union established to determine rates, the amount is flexible. A good basic rule is to use at least 10 percent of the total production price. It can be as little as 1 percent or as much as 50 percent, depending on the actual production itself and how much money can be committed to the production. If you are the producer you may be willing to take a smaller producer's fee in return for, say, a larger percentage of the distribution. Or, you may get repeat business if your fee is lower. There are countless reasons why the producer's fee may be less than 10 percent. For initial estimating, use this figure, and, as you gain experience, work from it.

The rest of the personnel costs are established by the unions and if the code books are read carefully and interpreted properly, your estimate will be accurate. The rates listed are the minimums established by the unions. This does not mean you are restricted to these amounts nor that someone can't demand overscale. This is particularly true of directors, D-O-P's, make-up artists, and hairdressers. These people, especially if they are well known and-or experienced and-or in great demand, can tell you their fees rather than your telling them. When preparing an estimate, weigh carefully the advantage to using a high-priced, well known, name director over a relatively unknown but equally qualified and much cheaper one. If you are restricted by a tight budget, this is one area where costs could be kept to at least union scale.

After you have totaled your production personnel costs, salary-wise, there are still some additional charges in this category. Each union has pension and welfare funds to which you must contribute and these amounts are computed in different ways: so much per hour, per day, per week, a flat fixed figure, or a percentage of gross earnings ranging from 5 to 15 percent. Also, some unions have vacation, scholarship, and apprentice funds to which the producer must contribute and these start at ½ to 1 percent and go up.

Also include a percentage of gross payroll to cover payroll taxes. This is roughly 12 percent. The percentage drops down to 5 percent for all payroll amounts that exceed the Social Security maximum. For example, assume that a producer makes $20,000. In your budget you would add 12 percent of $10,000 and 5 percent of 10,000 to your estimate. Check your local Social Security office for the exact dollar amount when FICA taxes are no longer withheld.

Your production personnel estimate will include, then, all salaries, pension and welfare contributions, and payroll taxes. The importance of reading and understanding the various union rulings can't be stressed enough. Don't ever guess at or assume anything. If there is any doubt as to the rulings, call the union business agent and ask for the correct interpretation. It might take you a while longer to prepare your estimate, but it will be accurate and there is less of a chance that you will be hit with hidden costs after your budget has been finalized.

Chapter 8
Talent

The two major unions involved in estimating the cost of performing talent are Screen Actors Guild (SAG) and American Federation of Television and Radio Artists (AFTRA). A third union, Screen Extras Guild (SEG), is active only on the West Coast. Before starting an AFTRA production, it is advisable to get a copy of the specific regulation (code) books for your local area. For example, if your production office is in Akron, Ohio, the code books applicable to your production would come from the Cleveland office. Call the local business agent and ask him for a set of pertinent code books. However, if your production is under SAG's jurisdiction, all code books are national, excluding those covering New York Extra Players.

When do you use AFTRA and when do you use SAG? Originally, it was very simple: anything shot on film was SAG; if it was done with electronic video equipment (video tape), it was AFTRA. Now, however, SAG also includes video tape.

The following are direct quotes from the AFTRA and SAG code books, respectively. AFTRA's jurisdiction includes any commercials, programs, or shows that "...are produced and recorded by means of any electronic video equipment (including a combination electronic and motion picture or 'slave' camera) used either in connection with television broadcasting or in connection with electronic video recording, whether by means of disc, wire, tape, kinescope, audio tape recorders, video tape recorders, wire recorders, disc recorders and any other apparatus now or hereaft＿ developed which is used to transmit, transfer, or record light or sound for immediate or eventual conversion into electrical energy. (Excluded from the foregoing are announcements recorded solely by motion picture camera not in connection with a television or radio broadcast)."

SAG's jurisdiction "...has always meant and included motion pictures whether made on or by film, tape, or otherwise and whether produced by means of motion picture cameras, electronic cameras or devices, tape devices, or any combination of the foregoing, or any other means, methods, or devices now used or which may hereafter be adopted..except only with respect to (any production) made by means of electronic tape or any other electronic device produced...by television stations or television networks using broadcasting studio facilities of such television stations or television networks.''

Early in your estimating, determine which union you will deal with. This must be done to know what rates are applicable and also for details such as travel time, meal penalties, overtime, wardrobe, etc. Also, if you are using a production house, find out if its members are signatories to either SAG or AFTRA and if you must use the union to which they are a signatory.

When preparing your estimate, notice that there are four ways to cast your production:

1. Outside casting service
2. Staff casting director
3. Agents
4. Do-it-yourself.

These methods range from expensive to economical, and the method you use depends upon the flexibility of your budget and the needs of the production.

OUTSIDE CASTING SERVICES

The most expensive and most efficient way is to hire an outside casting service. They prescreen all talent, attend all preproduction and production meetings, negotiate salaries, keep all records, pay all performing personnel (including agent's fees) as well as filing the necessary tax reports and union pension and welfare reports. Their fee for performing this service is usually a flat percentage of the total package; i.e., after all talent costs have been totaled, they will add 10, 15, 20 or even 25 percent to this figure for their service. The big advantage to using such a service is that they relieve you of a direct responsibility to the talent and liability for them, and handle the many details involving talent in the production. In addition, they have an intricate working knowledge of the union rules and regulations, as well as being well acquainted with the talent available in your area. When hiring a casting service, make sure they are reputable and recognized by SAG and AFTRA business agents.

STAFF CASTING DIRECTOR

Another approach to casting talent is to hire a staff casting director for the production. This is usually done for feature productions or television series. As with the outside casting service, the staff casting director is responsible for all phases of talent relationships from preliminary negotiations through to final reports of the talent unions. However, rather than charging a fee, the casting director is salaried and all talent expenses are paid by the production. Here, again, it is very important to have someone who is well versed in SAG and AFTRA rulings and who is known and respected by the union business agents. In your estimate, include all the figures for talent as prepared by the casting director plus his or her salary for the time involved. Remember to add 12 percent on top of the casting director's salary to cover payroll taxes for her.

AGENTS

The third method is to cast through agents. This takes more of your time and requires a thorough knowledge of union rules and regulations. However, it is cheaper. Here's how it works.

Whether you are working exclusively with one agent or several, the approach is the same. You explain your script or storyboard needs to them in the same way you would to a casting director. They then prescreen the talent and send you a selected few for each part. You have the casting sessions and from these make your decision. The agents usually do not estimate talent costs but will negotiate with the talent for you. The actual estimating must be done by you.

BUDGET CONSIDERATIONS

When preparing the budget, you should be aware of the following costs and include them where applicable (all are included in the code books for your production area):

a. **Session fees:** How many principals, extras, voice-overs, dancers, and singers are you using? How do you determine which category to use? Are there any star performers? Are you paying scale or over-scale?

b. **Overtime:** Do you anticipate 10-, 12-, or 14-hour days? If so, compute the amount of overtime involved for each performer at time-and-a-half or double-time, where applicable. You may find that three 8-hour days are more reasonable than two 12-hour days.

c. **Travel time:** If your production site is outside the "studio zone" travel time is computed. Check your local code books for the definition of the studio zone and the applicable radius. It varies with each area. ("Studio zone" is an area within a certain radius of a designated spot within a major metropolitan area. In Los Angeles, for example, it's 6 miles from Fifth and Rossmore Streets; in New York, 8 miles from Columbus Circle, etc.) How is travel time computed? What if you travel on Saturday, Sunday, or a legal holiday? Do you allow for meal periods? If your location site is so remote that traveling costs become prohibitive, consider a site closer to your production office.

d. **Wardrobe:** Who is providing the actors' clothing? You or the talent themselves? If talent provides it, how many changes are needed? The talent is reimbursed for each required outfit; check the code books for the rates for men and women, since they are different.

e. **Meal penalties:** Although these are not planned, if you study your production schedule closely, you may see times when a meal penalty will be unavoidable. Include $25 per half hour past the time allowed for a meal break. This applies to all talent.

f. **Fittings, wardrobe tests, make-up tests:** If the talent does not supply their own wardrobe and fittings are required, these must be included in the budget. How much time is involved and how many performers will need fittings? Is the talent needed for make-up and-or wardrobe tests? Are the tests scheduled on the same day as the shooting or on a separate day? These can affect your budget because the amounts vary.

g. **Night differential:** If your script needs call for a specific shot, there is no need to consider this item. If, on the other hand, night shooting occurs as a result of poor planning or poor direction, this must be included. Or, this could occur in one very long production day when a location site is available only for a certain time period. This amount is usually 10 percent of the hourly rate added to the hourly rate.

h. **Rehearsals:** How many days of rehearsal will be needed? What talent is involved in rehearsing? Is special training of a performer required? Are there any expenses involved in rehearsal time? These should be included in your estimate.

i. **Per diem, including traveling expenses:** How much is allowed per person for food and lodging on a daily basis? What kind of accommodations are required? As with the other unions, the union ruling is "first class" accommodations for lodging and traveling. Include all plane fares, train fares, automobile rentals, hotel and motel rooms, meals, etc., for talent only in this section.

j. **Saturday, Sunday, holiday work:** Is there a different pay scale for Saturday, Sunday, and holidays? What is it? What are the legal holidays? Check your production schedule closely to determine if you will be paying premium salaries for these days when your production could just as easily be handled during a normal week day.

k. **Flight insurance:** How many of your cast members will be flown to the location site? In your budget include $10 per performer for flight insurance.

l. **Payroll taxes:** How many performers will be paid through the payroll system and how many as independent contractors? Independent contractors are paid a flat fee. If they are paid on payroll, add 12 percent of the gross **salary** payment to your estimate for payroll taxes. This 12 percent is **not** part of wardrobe, fittings, flight insurance, or meal penalties; only of the salary earned for time spent in the production.

m. **Union pension and welfare contributions:** As with payroll taxes, this is a percentage of salaries earned by the performers and paid by the producer to the union (SAG or AFTRA) pension and welfare fund. It is equal to 6½ percent (as of this writing) of the total performer's salaries paid.

n. **Weather days:** Are some of your locations susceptible to unsuitable weather? Should you allow for the possibility of rain, snow, or fog? If there is any doubt in your mind, include sufficient monies in your budget to cover "weather permitting" calls.

o. **Agent's fees:** If your production is under AFTRA's jurisdiction, the agent's fees are 10 percent of the total session payment to the talent. This 10 percent is **added** to the payment and the cost is absorbed by your production. Under SAG's jurisdiction, the agent's fees are also 10 percent; however, this amount is paid by the actor himself and is **deducted** from his total session payment by the agent. Therefore, if you are using SAG, it is not necessary to include any amount in this category.

DO-IT-YOURSELF PRODUCTION

The fourth and least expensive way to cast your production is the "do-it-yourself" method. This way you contact the talent directly and handle all negotiations yourself. Where do you find the talent? Through talent indexes (in New York, Player's Guide; in Los Angeles, Academy Player's Directory. Check with your local business agent for your area), friends, local theatre groups, talent registries, acting schools, modeling schools, union membership rosters, placement of ads in the entertainment section of your local newspaper, etc. Unless you have an idea of where to begin your talent search and who you are looking for, this can be a very time-consuming job. It really depends on how tight your budget is. If your funds are limited this method is your only alternative.

If your production is done in the cinema verité style, the talent costs will be minimal. The people, non-actors, who appear in the production will have signed releases and are paid a nominal amount (see Chapter 10). The only other talent that might be involved would be a narrator. The length of the production will determine the amount to be paid to him. Assuming that only a narrator is used, the amounts to be included in your estimate would be a session fee, the agent's fee (if AFTRA), the pension and welfare contribution, and payroll taxes.

The main items in your talent estimate, then, are as follows:

1. Casting service
2. Casting director
3. Principals
4. Extras
5. Narrator/voice-over
6. Pension and welfare
7. Payroll taxes
8. Agent's fees
9. Wardrobe

10. Travel
11. Per diem
12. Miscellaneous.

Item 12, miscellaneous, covers flight insurance, fittings, weather contingency allotments, meal penalties, rehearsals, etc. In short, any costs that might be incurred which are not itemized.

COST CUTTING

Where can you save money in the talent area? First, through proper and efficient scheduling of your production. Make sure all scenes in the same location are shot at the same time, even if they do not appear in that particular sequence in the film. Second, set up a good, realistic production schedule; prepare your estimate from this schedule, and once production begins, stick to this schedule. Third, hire unknowns. If an actor or actress is considered a star, they can command higher salaries and, possibly, add hours to your shooting schedule. Fourth, pay the talent as independent contractors if they are incorporated. This way you save as much as 12 percent of their total salaries in payroll taxes. Fifth, as mentioned earlier, do the casting yourself.

In summary, then, how you prepare your talent estimate depends on the amount of money committed to the production. By far the easiest—and most expensive—is the outside casting service. However, if funds are limited, there are other alternatives. Contact the local SAG or AFTRA business agent in your production area. Get to know him. Request a set of code books so that you can become familiar with the various rulings. And prepare a realistic budget, taking into consideration the many cost areas that are involved.

Chapter 9
Scenic Elements

The many physical properties of a production are called scenic elements. This includes a full spectrum of visuals from set design and construction to hand props, graphics, wardrobe, costumes, etc.

Often a set designer or, on the West Coast, an art director, is hired to design and coordinate all the scenic elements of your production. He (or she) is similar to an architect, inasmuch as he not only designs the set but also makes blueprints with specifications to scale. Once this design has been approved, the set can be built. Set designers (ADs) are members of the United Scenic Artists union and usually charge on a daily basis. Sometimes they will charge a flat fee for a very long or time-consuming production. Call your local United Scenic Artists union office for the applicable daily rate in your area. Remember to include payroll taxes and pension and welfare payments if they are not being paid as independent contractors.

After design approval, there are two approaches to putting up the set. The cheaper of the two is to rent stock sets or set pieces. These are sets that have already been constructed and are available on a daily rental basis. Although this limits the creativity of your set, it is very inexpensive and readily available.

BUILDING A SET

The other alternative is to build your set to specifications. How big must the set be? How many men will be needed to build the set? How many days will it take? Does it need to be on casters? How much time will be needed to put the set up? Does the set have to be touched up once it is on stage? What type of set are you building? Does it contain a kitchen? Must it be a working kitchen? The answers to these questions will help you estimate the cost of your scenic elements more accurately.

In video tape, most sets are built outside the studio and trucked into the studio. In film, the sets are frequently constructed in the studio. In your estimate, be sure to include all trucking charges for moving the set. These charges are never less than $50 and often much more. Construction is figured on time and material and includes all the necessary manpower to build and install the set.

In addition to set construction, the set must be furnished according to the design. This includes large props, such as sofas, rugs, chairs, lamps, tables, cars, carriages, etc., and hand props such as dishes, silverware, fans, ashtrays, curtains, etc. In a union production, an outside prop man is hired to get these props. He alone, or with the designer, locates the props and arranges for their delivery to the studio. Outside prop men are hired per diem and, if there is sufficient money in your budget to pay one, an experienced prop man is an asset to your production because he knows where to get many unusual and otherwise hard-to-find props. In a low-budget or nonunion production, the production assistant can be responsible for propping the set. During actual production, you will need an inside prop man. This cost is included in your basic stage crew requirements (see Chapter 7).

Does your script call for any special effects? This includes breakaway glass, fire, flying rigs, fog, wind, flares, cobwebs, guns, etc. The charges for these specially constructed effects are included in the scenic elements section of your budget. In the case of fog, wind, or cobwebs, there are special machines that can be rented daily or weekly for this. Other effects may have to be specially constructed for your production. If so, the full cost of construction will be included in your budget, since it probably has a one-time-only use.

ART WORK

If your production has titles, credits, charts, graphs, or any form of art work, this must be included in the graphics charges. Are the titles hand-lettered or set in type? Are your credits on flip cards or a roll? Are you showing a map? Charts? Graphs? Are you shooting existing material or will there have to be an artist's rendition? Does your production have to be color corrected? (This can be quite expensive since it is often hand work done by an artist.) Color correcting is more common to commercials than any other form of production and is a catch-all phrase that includes any alteration of a package.

True color correcting means to alter the color of a package or portion of a package to compensate for the inability of a film or TV camera to accurately reproduce that color. For example, a client's blue package may look greenish when photographed by a certain film. To correct the situation, a dummy box would be made with a different shade of blue that, when photographed, would match the true blue of the box. Frequently, too, a client will want to remove some of the clutter from his package, i.e., price, size, etc. This has nothing to do with color but is usually lumped into the same category.

Almost every production needs title cards. These can cost from $25 each and up. In a low-budget production you may want to hand-letter your own titles. Although this is not as professional as type-set or artist-rendered cards, it is certainly cheaper. If the graphics in your production are extensive, consult a graphics designer when preparing your budget. He will help you prepare a more accurate cost estimate of the total graphics.

WARDROBE

What are the wardrobe requirements of your production? Is your production in modern dress or does it call for special period pieces or costumes? If special costumes are to be made, a costume designer must be hired who will both design and make the costumes. Depending upon the costuming needs of your production, this can be an expensive item. Costume designers are hired per diem and charge you for their creative time plus materials. A less expensive approach is to hire a stylist who dresses or costumes the production with ready-made outfits. The stylist can rent from a costume house or buy clothes from a store. A stylist coordinates the wardrobe of the performers including jewelry, shoes, accessories, hats, etc. Stylists belong to the United Scenic Artists union and can cost $100 a day and up. These charges, plus the cost of all clothing and accessories, are included in your estimate. The least expensive way to costume your production is to make each performer responsible for his or her own wardrobe. If the wardrobe requirements are for current dress, the costs are kept to a minimum (see Chapter 8).

CUE CARDS OR TELEPROMPTER

If your performers do not memorize their lines, it will be necessary to use cue cards or a teleprompter. Of the two, cue cards are cheaper. The cards cost approximately $1 each and can be lettered by the production assistant. Bear in mind, though, that an extra stagehand must be included in your budget to turn the cue cards for the performers. Teleprompting, which does not require an extra stagehand, is more expensive than cue cards and is available on an hourly basis. Include two additional hours for set up and strike in your estimate.

TRUCKING

One of the biggest items in a union production is trucking. The sets, big props, rugs and appliances, and equipment must be trucked in and out; in short, anything that you are using on stage or on location must be delivered by union truck drivers. This is expensive and necessary when shooting an all-union production or if you are shooting in a unionized studio. Never budget less than $150 for trucking in a union production. Many times it will be much more.

MISCELLANEOUS

In every production, you will have miscellaneous charges. Maybe the floor of the studio needs to be painted. You must pay for scenic artists to paint the floor and then, when the production is finished, the floor must be repainted to its original color. The scenic artists charge on an hourly basis, plus you must pay for the paint. Does your hair stylist need a hair dryer? Rental, plus trucking, fits into miscellaneous. Do the actors need risers to raise them up? That's a miscellaneous charge. Anything that doesn't fit into a specific category goes into miscellaneous, of course.

Scenic elements, then, are the many visuals in your production. They include set design and construction, graphics, props, special effects, costumes and costume design, wardrobe, color correction, and stylists. Since this section of your budget can be as much as one-fourth of your total production price, make sure it is accurate. When in doubt about any facet, consult with an expert. Usually, he will give you advice freely in return for the opportunity of working on your production.

Chapter 10
Location Expenses

Unless your production is shot in a studio in the immediate vicinity of your production office, there will be location expenses. These are broken down into nine categories:

1. Transportation
2. Food (per diem)
3. Lodging (per diem)
4. Vehicle rentals
5. Mileage
6. Shipping
7. Location-release fees
8. Travel time (including pension and welfare, and payroll taxes)
9. Miscellaneous

TRANSPORTATION

In the transportation area, include all train and airplane fares for your crew to all locations. Oftentimes, if your budget is limited, it is to your advantage to take only key production personnel with you, i.e. director, producer, and first cameraman, and to use local people for the balance of your crew. If you are using all union personnel, be sure to check the various union rulings before making any travel arrangements. Since most unions call for "first class accommodations," this area of your budget can become quite expensive if you are transporting a large union crew.

FOOD

The majority of the union rules state that if you travel over 25 miles from your home office to the location site, a certain amount of money must be given each crew member for his meals. Since union rules vary from city to city, it would be impossible to use specific figures in this chapter for per diem. (Per day. Refers to a specified amount paid to each crew member for food and lodging for the day, depending upon the distance from the home office.) Therefore, we'll use a hypothetical figure that is about average, which as of this writing, is $15 a day. This is the amount to be used in computing the figures for the "food" category. Count every crew member and the number of days each must be paid per diem. If your production schedule calls for your crew to be on location for an extended period of time, seriously consider taking only key personnel, as mentioned earlier, and hiring local technicians. Before preparing a final estimate, be sure to check with the local union offices to get the exact per diem figures that are applicable to your production. (For nonunion production, see Chapter 16.) Also included in this category should be any catering of meals that may be required (see Chapter 11).

LODGING

For lodging, as for food, be sure to check with the local union business managers for the amount that must be paid. As with travel, requirements are for "first class accommodations"; this translates into one person to a room. If you are preparing a preliminary estimate and don't have time to verify the various union requirements, use $20 per day per man. With this figure you can begin to prepare your estimate in order to get a "ballpark" figure. However, when it is being refined, be sure you have confirmed the exact amounts with the various locals. (For nonunion production, see Chapter 16.)

VEHICLE RENTALS

Automobile rentals must be included when on location. The use of cars must be figured from arrival at the airport or train station until departure. It is advisable to get rates from two or three competitive companies and keep these figures handy in an estimating reference book. If these figures are not immediately available, allow four men to a car and use, as a base figure, $25 per day per car. Include mileage if there will be extensive traveling while on location (over 100 miles a day for each car). If each car covers less than this daily, the $25 figure in your estimate will be sufficient. Other vehicle rentals to be included are make-up and dressing room vans, when needed, and portable sanitation facilities (comfort stations).

MILEAGE

Mileage refers to monies paid to personnel who use their cars for the purposes of the production. Oftentimes, if your location is within 100 miles of your production office, it is advisable to have the individuals involved use their own cars rather than arranging for rental cars or public transportation. Depending upon the unions involved and in what part of the country you are shooting, this figure could range from 10 to 20 cents a mile. As with per diem, check with the local union business managers to get the specific amounts. Also include sufficient money in this category for tolls, when needed.

SHIPPING

If you are traveling any distance from your production headquarters, you may have to consider shipping some of the equipment if it is not available near the location site or if it is special equipment that must be transported from your production office. In this case, you must include shipping charges in your estimate. Always have at least $100 in your estimate and, if you have to ship a great quantity of cameras, lights, etc., be sure to get quotes from the airlines as to specific charges, including insurance.

If you are shooting outside of the United States, custom charges are to be included in your estimate. There is no charge for shipping raw stock out of the country (film, ¼-inch tape or video tape). However, if the film or tapes are exposed or used, there is a charge when returning to the United States. In order to get this material processed, it is necessary to use a Custom House broker. He will handle the details necessary to get the material out of and into the country. In your estimate, figure .0065 cents per foot for all exposed film, .007 cents per foot for ¼-inch tape, and .005 cents per foot for video tape.

To avoid paying customs or duty on anything you take out of the country, be sure to file a registration form with Customs on all equipment and raw stock that you are taking out of the United States. If some of your stock is unexposed when you return, there is no charge for bringing it back into the United States, as long as you declared it initially on your registration form. If you do not declare all raw stock, as well as equipment, when leaving the country, your import duties can be astronomical when re-entering the United States. Before leaving the United States, contact a Custom House broker or local Customs officer to obtain the necessary forms to be filled out. Also, obtain the necessary foreign permits for the countries in which you are shooting.

Location: _____

Producer: _____

Date: _____

In consideration of One ($1.00) Dollar, to me in hand paid by _____ (Producer) _____,

the receipt of which is hereby acknowledged, I, the undersigned, being of legal

age and having read this release before having signed it, do hereby release

_____ (Producer) _____ and/or _____ (Sponsor) _____ from any and all

claims which I may have by reason of the showing of my name or picture and I

hereby grant, sell and release all right, title and interest I may have in said pic-

tures to _____ (Producer) _____ and to its successors or assigns.

_____

Witness:

_____

If participant is a minor:

_____

Parent, Legal Guardian

Fig. 10-1. Typical performing release form.

LOCATION-RELEASE FEES

If your location is gratis, you do not need to include any figure in the area of location fees. If, on the other hand, there is a charge, be sure this is in your budget (see Chapter 2). Release fees are included if you anticipate having people appear in your production who are not cast members but who are identifiable. The standard release (Fig. 10-1) pays each participant $1. Be sure to include an adequate amount in your budget, especially if your production is being shot in a heavily populated area and there is a strong chance that some of the people will accidentally appear in the film. If you don't pay release fees, you run the risk of being sued for a sizable amount of money by any of the participants that were not legally released and who are easily identified.

TRAVEL TIME

If you are budgeting a union production, it is necessary to pay travel time for all personnel. Again, check the rulings for this payment with the business managers of the various locals involved in your production. Will it be necessary to travel on a Saturday, Sunday, or holiday? Are these days straight time, time-and-a-half, or double-time days? How long will the personnel be traveling? Must they be paid for a minimum of 4 hours, 8 hours, only for actual time traveling, or portal-to-portal? (Door to door. This means from the time they leave their residence until they arrive at the location site or lodging accommodations.) Is there a meal allowance? As you can begin to see, the more accurate and well thought out your pre-production schedule, the more accurate your estimate will be. Be sure to add 12 percent payroll taxes to this amount, plus the applicable pension and welfare contributions. If your production is nonunion, this area could be eliminated if you have negotiated all-inclusive flat fees for the total production.

MISCELLANEOUS

The miscellaneous category covers all expenses for which there is no specific listing. It includes petty cash for cabs, laundry, gratuities, etc. For example, if a doorman or policeman has been particularly helpful in aiding your production, a tip is advisable. In addition, there are always incidentals that cannot be anticipated. The figure entered into miscellaneous should be at least $200 or 1 percent of your total below-the-line budget, whichever is greater.

Location expenses cover, then, all expenses incurred outside a studio that relate directly to the location and the personnel involved. It includes the transportation of all production personnel by airplane, train, or automobile. The amount of money to be budgeted for per diem expenses varies from union to union. Before finalizing your estimate, be sure to check with the business managers of the locals involved to verify the exact figures. Also check if the rulings state "first class accommodations" and how travel time is budgeted. If your production is traveling outside the United States, include all required customs charges and, prior to departure, file all required forms far enough in advance to avoid any penalties or excess charges.

If your production estimate is too high, there are three major areas in which you can cut location expenses. First, shoot nonunion; you are not obligated by union rulings to pay a specific amount. Second, stay within a 25-mile radius of your production office. This will save money in transportation, food and lodging costs. Third, if you must travel any distance to a location, take only the key personnel with you and hire local production talent.

Chapter 11
Survey

If your production is done entirely in a studio, there is no need for a survey; it is only when locations are involved that a survey must be included in your estimate of production costs. Ideally, you should do a survey **before** preparing an estimate, since it will give you an exact idea of the many cost areas that will be involved in the production. However, this is seldom possible because a survey is done **after** the budget has been approved and the job awarded to a specific producer.

What is a survey? Why do you need one? How does it become a cost item in your budget? When preparing your estimate, consider the number of locations and how far they are from your production office. Who will be doing your survey? Will you send the producer, director, and-or director of photography? In film, usually the director and the D-O-P do the survey. In tape, either your producer or director goes plus the lighting director (LD) and technical director (TD).

How many locations are to be surveyed and how long will it take? When preparing an estimate, the survey costs should include the following figures:

1. The number of days each man will be gone, multiplied by his daily rate plus pension and welfare contributions and 12 percent payroll taxes.

2. Per diem expenses for each man for the number of days they are gone.

3. Transportation for each member of the survey crew to all locations (remember, union rules call for first-class facilities).

4. Auto rentals where necessary and-or mileage.

5. A small miscellaneous amount to cover cabs, gratuities, telephone calls, laundry, etc.

For example, suppose your production office is located in New York City and you have a film script with four locations:

Philadelphia, New York City, Boston, Los Angeles. A survey is needed in all the areas to find the right production location, facilities, and personnel, as well as available accommodations for the cast and crew. Assuming that your survey team will spend one day at each location and that the producer, director, and D-O-P will be making the survey, the amount budgeted for the survey would break down as follows:

Producer, 4 days at $100 per day	$400.00
Director, 4 days at $150 per day	600.00
D-O-P, 4 days at $200 per day	800.00
P & W (D-O-P & director)	50.00
12 percent payroll taxes	216.00
Travel: Philadelphia via auto ($25 per day + 200 miles at .15 per mile)	55.00
New York via auto ($25 per day + 100 miles at .15 per mile)	40.00
Boston via airplane; $16 per round trip X 3	48.00
Los Angeles via airplane; $310 per round trip X3	930.00
Auto rentals: Boston and Los Angeles, $25 per day + 125 miles at .05 per mile each	80.00
Per diem: 3 men at $35 per day for 2 days (Los Angeles and Boston)	210.00
Per diem: 3 men at $15 per day for 2 days (Philadelphia and New York)	90.00

(The above per diem figures are average. Check the rulings of the specific unions involved to get exact amounts.)

Miscellaneous	50.00

Total survey estimate: $3,569.00

The above total is the amount you would put into your budget, if you are estimating a union production. In a nonunion production, this amount would be lower because there would be no pension and welfare contributions and your survey team could travel coach class. After the job has been accepted (union or nonunion), the amount could be lowered somewhat if the director and-or producer include the survey in their overall price. This is negotiable. However, do not make this bargain with the production people involved. You could end up losing money.

LOCATION CONSIDERATIONS

When surveying a location, the first question to be answered is: Who is your major contact at the location site; who is the person with ultimate authority? Once the proper contact has been established and permission granted, it is advisable to draw up a brief letter of agreement outlining the use of the location and the commitment of the location owner. If this is not done, you are taking a chance on there being a misunderstanding as to use, dates, etc. This will cost you money in downtime (actually, time where manpower or equipment is not being used to its fullest; nonproductive time as a result of faulty equipment, late arrivals, forgotten props, etc.). Once the job has been awarded and the survey taken, your budget can be refined, cost-wise.

When surveying a location, always check the availability of electrical power. Is it sufficient for the needs of your production or will you have to bring a generator? This can boost your production cost, because not only must you include the price of the generator but also the costs of the men to drive and run it.

Are there any neighborhood restrictions? For example, if you want to shoot a night scene and there can be no disturbing noises between 11 PM and 6 AM, your schedule might have to be altered to adhere to the neighborhood restrictions. Or, you may have to get special permission from the police department.

Is your location in a heavily congested area? Will you need parking facilities? Again, you may have to contact the local police department to arrange for special street parking. In New York City, for example, it is necessary to obtain a location permit from the Chamber of Commerce, prior to shooting, so that "no parking" signs can be posted and the police alerted to your production plans. The charge for this permit is usually $25. However, the rules and regulations for each area vary, so always check first; don't assume anything. If the police are alerted to your production plans far enough in advance, they will assign policemen specifically to you for directing traffic, re-routing pedestrians, etc. As with anyone else, the earlier they are notified, the more prepared they will be and the more cooperative.

How accessible is your location? What are the loading and unloading facilities? Consider where you are shooting, the type of equipment you are using, and how it will be transported to the site. It may be that a couple of jeeps or land rovers would have to be included in your estimate to facilitate transportation of your equipment and personnel.

If your location is a remote one, what arrangements have you made for feeding the cast and crew? Will they be able to find a suitable restaurant nearby or will the meals have to be brought in to you? In some major production areas, there are special mobile van units that cater specifically to production crews. Again, this is an expense item that should be listed in your budget. (Refer to Chapter 10.)

Are there make-up artists, wardrobe handlers, hairdressers, or home economists in your budget? If so, are there sufficient facilities for them? If not, include trucks for wardrobe, hair and make-up in your estimate, as well as kitchen facilities for the home economist, where needed, and portable dressing rooms. Include the number of trucks and total use days in your budget, as well as payment to the drivers (if teamsters are used) and the mileage to and from the location site.

To reiterate, the main purpose of a survey is to eliminate as many problems **prior** to production as possible. The fewer the problems, the smoother the production, and the easier it will be to adhere to your original estimate. A survey should not be treated cursorily because it can ultimately save you money.

Chapter 12

Editing

Since this is not a technical manual, there will be no attempt to describe the functions and uses of the various types of editing equipment and supplies; our purpose is only to alert you to the cost areas to be considered in the area of editing.

VIDEO TAPE

Estimating the charges for editing a video tape production is easier than for film. Since tape is edited electronically, you don't need as great an amount of editing supplies as you do for film which is edited physically. However, since video tape equipment is so much more expensive than film, it cannot be rented in the same manner. Instead of renting all equipment from a supply house and setting up the editing facilities yourself, your editing will have to be done at a production or service facility that owns the needed equipment and has it available on an hourly basis. The rental price includes the equipment plus the necessary technical personnel to run it. Fig. 12-1 is a typical video tape editing rate card. Since the production facility hires the personnel, you do not become directly involved in union rulings and regulations, as this is handled by them. It is only important to know that you are dealing with IATSE, NABET or IBEW and that the rulings discussed in Chapter 7 are applicable here.

When preparing your estimate, determine how many video tape recorders are needed and how long you will need them. Although most editing is done electronically, there are several different methods of preparation for editing. You can edit A and B rolls, as in film, and mix that way. This would require three VTRs, two for playback and one for record. You can edit film and tape at the same time. This would take at least two VTRs (one playback and one record) and a film chain (telecine). Or, you can edit scene by scene with a random selection of what was shot. This would take at least two VTRs, one playback and one record. Although it is possible to edit physically, as in film, it is not recommended.

The general rule to use when estimating the time needed to edit electronically is to figure an average of 15 minutes per

VIDEO TAPE MIXING

(All mixes include slate camera with title stand and control room)

A&B tape mixes (2 VTR-PB, 1 VTR-Rec)	300.00 per hr.
A&B film/tape (1 VTR-PB, 1 Telecine, 1 VTR-Rec)	325.00 per hr.
A&B film (2 Telecine, 1 VTR-Rec)	350.00 per hr.
A&B film with magnetic audio (2 Telecine, 1 VTR-Rec, 1 mag. dubber)	375.00 per hr.
Additional VTRs, each	100.00 per hr.
Additional magnetic dubbers, each	25.00 per hr.

Up to ¼-hr. set-up is allowed; minimums on each use, ½-hr.

FILM TO VIDEO TAPE TRANSFERS

Composite (1 Telecine, 1 VTR-Rec, title camera and stand)	225.00 per hr.
Interlock (1 Telecine. 1 VTR-Rec, 1 mag. dubber, title camera and stand)	250.00 per hr.
Up to ¼-hr. set-up is allowed; minimums on each use, ½-hr.	
Overtime, in addition to mixing rates above, per man-hour	25.00
Additional set-up or stand-by time, per clock-hour	150.00

ELECTRONIC EDITING

Computer editing with two VTRs	300.00 per hr.
Editec or Edicomp editing with two VTRs	200.00 per hr.
Additional machines or Ampex HS-200 disc recorder	100.00 per hr.
Up to ¼-hr. set-up is allowed; minimums on each use, ½-hr.	
Overtime, in addition to editing rates above, per man-hour	25.00
Additional set-up or stand-by time, per clock-hour	150.00

Courtesy of Reeves Video

Fig. 12-1. Video tape editing rate card.

edit; therefore, if you have 20 edits you would need five hours of machine time plus another 15 minutes for machine set up. If the cuts are complicated, add more time; if simple, less. Add more time, too, if there are three or more VTRs involved, if film is interwoven with the tape, or there is a complicated special effect. The kinds of special effects will determine what equipment is to be rented. Simple effects can be handled by a mixer; more complicated ones by the slow-motion machine (Ampex HS 100) or the more elaborate version of this equipment, the Ampex HS 200, which will allow you to animate and edit frame by frame on video tape. As with the charges for the VTRs, the prices listed by the production facility include all the technical manpower required to operate the equipment.

It is impossible to give you an idea of how long, in hours or days, it will take to edit a video tape production into its completed form without an explanation of the concept. You cannot apply the same "rule of thumb" to video tape that you can to film. The only rule that is fairly accurate is the one of 15 minutes per edit.

The charges in your estimate will include any or all of the following:

The number of VTRs multiplied by the hourly charge (this includes the engineer's service), plus setup time.

A film chain (telecine), when needed
Slow-motion machines (HS 100, HS 200)
Title stand
Slate camera
Mixer
Editec or Edicomp
Video tape stock
Reels and boxes
Overtime for engineers.

FILM EDITING

Film editing is more complicated but also more flexible. In addition to working through a full production facility, as with video tape, you also have the option to use an editing service or handle the coordination of the editing yourself.

As a beginner, use the following rule in estimating total editing time:

Commercial (16mm or 35mm) with union or nonunion personnel: 10 days.

Half-hour show (16 or 35) with union personnel: 8 weeks.

Half-hour show (16 or 35) with nonunion personnel: 7 weeks.

One-hour show (16 or 35) with union personnel: 20 weeks.

One hour show (16 or 35) with nonunion personnel: 16 weeks.

Feature (16 or 35) with union or nonunion personnel: Minimum 6 months.

These are averages and will vary with the complexity or simplicity of your production.

There are three unions to be considered: NABET, IATSE, and IBEW. If you are having union personnel edit the production, call the business agent of the local you will be using and ask for a copy of the current contracts. In addition to daily and weekly rates, these contracts will outline the working conditions in the same manner as discussed in Chapter 7. The union contracts will give you the minimum wages to be paid. Many experienced editors, though, are paid over scale. The union contracts are just a guideline for scale salaries.

Estimate the number of days or weeks it will take to edit your production and use that figure for computing all editing salaries. Figure at least one editor, one assistant editor, and one apprentice editor. The editor cuts the show according to continuity and works closely with the director. The assistant editor sets up the coding, puts sound track and picture in synchronization, acts as a lab liaison, and makes out the log and camera reports. The apprentice editor sorts and stores all the material, labels cans, mends and repairs film, and handles the many little details that the editor and assistant editor don't have time to do. Estimate all three for the entire editing period.

There are other classifications of editors: dubbing editor, title editor, music editor, effects editor, etc. These, however, are germane only to the West Coast. If you are working in California, study the union contract carefully to see if any of these must be included in your budget.

If an editing service is used, they will quote a price that should include all editors, room and equipment, and editing supplies. When you coordinate the editing yourself, these costs will have to be itemized on your budget.

Determine what type of editing equipment will be needed; this will help you figure out what size rooms to rent. The three major types of editing machines are the Moviola (16 and 35), the Steenbeck (16 and 35), and the KEM. If you are unfamiliar with how each functions or which is best for your production, ask your editor which he (or she) prefers. How many machines will you need? For how long? Is it cheaper to rent or buy?

When negotiating for editing space, bear in mind how much equipment will be going into the area, how many people will be working, what the power supply is, and how accessible it is to the lab. For example, editing a 10-minute short would take fewer people and less equipment than an hour-long documentary; therefore, a smaller working area is needed. In New York, $50 a week is a reasonable amount to estimate for space. This should include a telephone.

What kind of accessory equipment and supplies should be included in your budget? Some or all of the following are necessary:

Editing table(s)
Editing chair(s)
Rewinds (hand or electric)
Trim bin
Hand truck
Racks
Viewing system (example: Moviescope)
Sound reader
Synchronizer
Siemens projector
Splicer (guillotine or butt)
Editing lamp
Clamps
Flange
Magnifying glass
Tight-wind adapter
Boxes for "outtakes" and trims
Reels
Razor blades
Cans
Split reels and cores
Gloves
Scissors
Splicing tape (clear and white)
¼-inch masking tape
Tape dispenser
A velvet
Cores
Kum Cleans
Grease pencils
Glue
Leader (white, black, exposed, developed).

Sometimes room rental will include these items; however, make sure you get an itemized list of everything that is included to be sure nothing is left out. When in doubt as to what equipment to get, ask your editor. Also, should you rent or buy? For a preliminary estimate, $75 a week is a reasonable figure to use for these supplies and the miscellaneous equipment.

To help in your compilation of costs, use a local editing equipment catalogue as a guideline (see Fig. 12-2). Notice the rates are daily, weekly, and monthly. In addition, most rental houses will give you long-term rates, which can be as much as 25 percent off the monthly rate card price. Some rental

MOVIOLA FILM EDITING MACHINES

	Daily	Weekly	Monthly (4 weeks)
Basic 16mm or 35mm. Complete w/composite picture sound head, separate optical/magnetic sound w/take-up arms.	$20.00	$60.00	$150.00
with One picture head, two sound heads	25.00	75.00	200.00
One picture head, three sound heads	35.00	105.00	315.00
One picture head, four sound heads	45.00	135.00	400.00
Two picture heads, one sound head	30.00	90.00	250.00
Two picture heads, two sound heads	40.00	120.00	300.00
Two picture heads, three sound heads	60.00	150.00	450.00
Three picture heads, one sound head (One week minimum)		160.00	480.00
Three picture heads, two sound heads (One week minimum)		180.00	540.00

MOVIOLA ACCESSORIES

	Daily	Weekly	Monthly (4 weeks)
Moviola 16mm or 35mm Silent Picture head only (Table Top model)	10.00	40.00	90.00
Moviola 16mm or 35mm sound head only	5.00	20.00	50.00
Add-A-Unit extension plate only (to add sound head)	3.00	12.00	30.00
Moviola film rack and bag	.25	1.00	2.50
Headset	1.00	4.00	10.00
TV Matte (cut-off mask)	.25	1.00	2.50
1.85:1 Matte	.25	1.00	3.00
Cinemascope Attachment	1.00	4.00	10.00

SYNCHRONIZERS

	Daily	Weekly	Monthly (4 weeks)
Single or double gang (16mm or 35mm)	2.00	8.00	20.00
Three or four gang (16mm or 35mm)	3.00	12.00	30.00
Five or six gang (16mm or 35mm)	5.00	20.00	50.00
Combination 1/16-1/35 w/two counters	2.50	10.00	25.00
Combination 2/16-2/35 w/two counters	3.50	14.00	35.00
Moviola motor drive synchronizer attachment	5.00	20.00	50.00
Magnetic Synchronizer attachment	1.00	4.00	10.00
Amplifier/speaker for magnetic synchronizer attachment	2.00	8.00	20.00
Mixer unit 2-4 inputs	1.00	4.00	10.00

VIEWERS

	Daily	Weekly	Monthly (4 weeks)
16mm Moviola Viewer	5.00	20.00	50.00
16mm Zeiss Moviscop, left to right	2.00	8.00	20.00
16mm Zeiss Moviscop, right to left	3.00	12.00	30.00
Craig or Bell & Howell Viewer	1.00	4.00	10.00
35mm large 4 x 6 screen viewer	5.00	20.00	50.00
ACE rotary viewer	2.00	8.00	20.00
ACE rotary viewer w/image erector	2.25	9.00	22.50
Precision viewer	2.00	8.00	20.00

SOUND READERS

	Daily	Weekly	Monthly (4 weeks)
Precision optical or magnetic	5.00	20.00	50.00
Precision combination optical and magnetic	7.50	30.00	75.00
Precision reader-viewer base plate	1.00	4.00	10.00
Precision optical or magnetic reader complete w/base plate and Zeiss viewer	10.00	40.00	100.00
Moviola SRO optical sound reader	3.00	12.00	30.00
Moviola SRM magnetic sound reader	2.00	8.00	20.00
Moviola SRC optical and magnetic sound reader	5.00	20.00	50.00
Moviola UHS amplifier (4" speaker)	2.00	8.00	20.00
Moviola UROM amplifier (6" speaker)	3.00	12.00	30.00

SPLICERS-Cement

	Daily	Weekly	Monthly (4 weeks)
Griswold 16mm or 35mm	$ .50	$2.00	$5.00
Maier-Hancock 8/16mm hot splicer	2.00	8.00	20.00
Maier-Hancock super 8 hot splicer	3.00	12.00	30.00
Maier-Hancock 16/35mm hot splicer	4.00	16.00	40.00
Stanco 8/16mm automatic	2.00	8.00	20.00

SPLICERS-Tape

	Daily	Weekly	Monthly (4 weeks)
Guillotine CIR 16mm or 35mm (straight or diagonal)	2.00	8.00	20.00
Rivas 16mm or 35mm (straight or diagonal)	2.00	8.00	20.00
HFC 16mm or 35mm (straight or diagonal)	2.00	8.00	20.00
Splicing blocks 16mm or 35mm	.50	2.00	5.00

REWINDS

	Daily	Weekly	Monthly (4 weeks)
Single or double reel, (per pair)	1.00	4.00	10.00
Four reel (per pair)	1.50	6.00	15.00
Differential rewinds, 2 way (each)	4.00	16.00	30.00
4 way (each)	8.00	32.00	75.00
Power rewind (each)	6.00	24.00	50.00
Tightwind adapter	.25	1.00	2.50
Formica rewind board	.50	2.00	5.00
No charge for spacers, spring clamps, or locks when ordered w/rewinds			

MISCELLANEOUS EDITING EQUIPMENT

	Daily	Weekly	Monthly (4 weeks)
Camart Editing Tables 28 x 60 w/light-well	2.50	10.00	25.00
28 x 60 no light-well	2.00	8.00	20.00
28 x 48 w/light-well	2.00	8.00	20.00
28 x 48 no light-well	1.50	6.00	15.00
Back rack (3 tiers)	.50	2.00	5.00
Editing stools (metal)	.50	2.00	5.00
Editing chairs, padded, swivel type	1.00	4.00	10.00
Camart floor rack (6 tiers)	1.50	6.00	15.00
Camart editing bin w/pin rack and liner	1.00	4.00	10.00
Stop watch (click-silent)	.60	2.00	5.00
Electric film timer 16 or 35mm	1.00	4.00	10.00
Numbering cue or bloop punch (each)	.50	2.00	5.00
Film reels to 2000 ft. capacity	.10	.50	1.00
Split reels	.25	1.00	2.50
Flanges	.50	2.00	5.00
Trombolite for editing table	1.00	4.00	10.00
Luxo lamp	1.00	4.00	10.00

Courtesy of The Camera Mart, Inc.

Fig. 12-2. Film editing rate card.

facilities offer leasing with an option to buy; others will consider buying back equipment that was purchased for a specific production. Insurance coverage should be provided by the producer (see Chapter 14).

A negative cutter is employed when the workprint is approved and ready to go to the lab for the optical negative or internegative and answer print. You can hire a negative cutter, use a service, have the lab do it or, as an absolute last resort and only if your budget is so tight you have no other choice, do it yourself. The prices are fairly standardized and the charges are based on 10-minute reels. Since most commercials are done optically, this function would not have to be included in a commercial estimate. However, if you are cutting the negative for a commercial, there is usually a minimum charge of at least $50.

As with the other categories involving payroll, include 12 percent of the gross payroll for taxes and allow sufficient monies to cover pension and welfare contributions to the unions. Since these amounts vary across the country, check with the local union business agent to get the exact amounts.

The miscellaneous category should be an amount approximately 5 percent of your total editing estimate. This covers any screenings prior to answer print, additional transfers, scratch track for purposes of editing, repairs on the editing equipment, or trucking. It covers any unforeseen charges or incidentals that were not originally planned.

HIRING AN EDITOR

How and where do you hire an editor? If it is a union production, the union office can give you a list of available editors. Otherwise, you must resort to friends, competitors, run an ad in the trade papers, and watch the credits on television and in theatres.

Video tape editorial costs include all personnel and equipment needed to produce the edited master. Film editing charges include all editorial personnel, equipment, supplies, and room rentals to take your production from the dailies stage to completed workprint through negative cutting.

Chapter 13
Opticals &
Animation

In the total production process, opticals and animation are usually considered post production activities. In a video tape production, opticals such as split screens, wipes, etc., can be incorporated during production if you are using multiple cameras and have a switcher. Otherwise, it is done during the mix (see Chapter 12). In film, though, the process is different.

OPTICAL EFFECTS

Opticals are usually subcontracted to a separate production facility—an optical house—and are as important a part of your production as the actual filming. An optical house serves two functions. First, it can enhance your existing material with an infinite variety and combination of effects (Fig. 13-1). Although most labs are able to do simple fades and dissolves, anything more complicated than that must be done by an optical house. The effects most often used are those that provide transitions from one scene to another such as fades, dissolves, and wipes. Other effects are split screen, matte photography, titles, charts, graphs, slow motion, freeze frame, anamorphic photography, superimposures, fast motion, etc. In an optical house, your production is actually re-shot to include these various effects.

The second function of an optical facility is corrective. Sometimes, after screening the dailies, the producer discovers certain shots missing, possibly necessitating a reshoot. In these instances, an optical house can take the existing footage and reshoot it during the optical printing, saving much money in studio or location shooting charges. For example, if a closeup is desired and there are only medium and long shots, the optical printer can make a closeup; the scene can be flopped over and the action reversed on the screen; bad composition at the edge of a frame can be eliminated by enlarging the frame and blowing up to size the portion of the

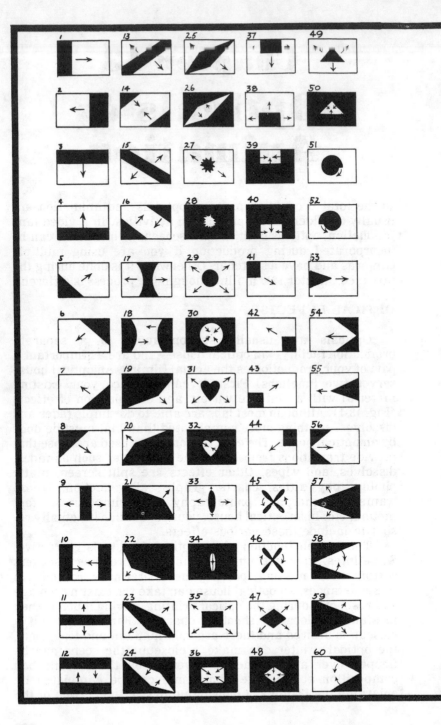

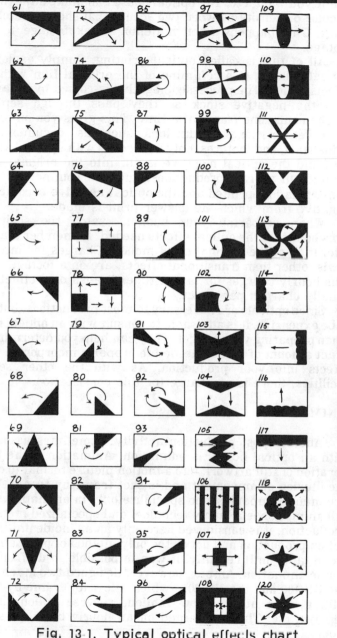

Fig. 13-1. Typical optical effects chart.
Courtesy of Coastal Film Service, Inc.

frame you want, etc. The optical house can make adjustments in color or density between two scenes that should match but don't. This happens when matching stock footage to new footage.

All of this is called optical printing. Simply explained, optical printing is a refilming of the original film with new effects added. The processed negative is copied by a camera onto the negative stock as they pass through separate mechanisms, one frame at a time. This gives you an optical negative. In long productions such as documentaries, industrials, and features, only the scenes with opticals are re-shot and the optical negative is cut into the original to be printed. In shorter productions, such as commercials, the entire film is reprinted and the optical negative becomes the negative from which the answer print is made.

When preparing your budget, watch the script or storyboard for the optical effects needed. Remember that any alteration of the original costs money. Charges for most op-ticals, other than transitional effects, are on a footage basis, plus hourly charges for layout time. Transitional effects are usually charged per effect.

Since opticals are necessary to most productions, but tend to be expensive, it is advisable to consult with an optical house when preparing your budget. They can help you determine the exact amount of money needed to properly incorporate these effects into your production. As with the other service facilities, there is no charge for this consultation.

ANIMATION

Another post production activity, sometimes associated with an optical house, is animation. Animation is the incor-poration of still artwork into a motion picture format to create the illusion of movement and is shot frame by frame. There are many companies who specialize only in animation. Since full animation is a highly technical and specialized method of production, it is considered here only as an incidental to live-action production and not as the only method of production. In video tape, until recently, it was impossible to do frame-by-frame animation. Ampex, however, designed two machines— the HS 100 and the HS 200—which allow for frame-by-frame editing, stop action, slow motion, reverse action, instant replays, etc. This is charged on an hourly basis, plus tape stock.

In film, animation can either be separate from live action or superimposed over it. In either instance, the initial preparation is the same. Still artwork is prepared with separate "cells" (drawings) for each frame of action. These cells are then put on the animation stand. This is a table with a camera mounted over it, facing down. Movement is achieved by moving either the camera or the table, or both, up, down, and sideways. These movements, coupled with the single-frame shooting and the changing artwork, give the effect of motion.

Animation is shot in both 16mm and 35mm. Animation charges are difficult to estimate and vary greatly with production needs. The greater the amount of realism needed, the more expensive it is. The number and type of characters will affect the price, too. A simple stick figure is certainly cheaper than a full-scale Walt Disney-type Cinderella. And if the animated figures must be in lip sync, the charges will be higher.

Animation is charged on a footage basis and can cost from $50 to $200 a foot, depending on the needs of your particular production. As you can imagine, 60 seconds of full animation in 35mm could run as high as $18,000 in just production costs. In addition, there are creative costs. These figures apply to titles, credits, charts, and graphs, too.

Another form of animation is computerized. There are no cells; instead, the animation is done electronically by a computer and filmed or taped as it happens. A great number of effects can be achieved without having an extensive amount of artwork made. However, you are limited to basic shapes and forms, since the process has not been refined enough to produce figures, multi-planed scenes, animals, etc. It is exceptionally good for titles and credits. Computer animation is available in the major production markets and is charged on an hourly basis.

When titles are put into your production they are "burned in." This is actually a combination of matte photography with artwork to achieve the end result of titles and credits over existing footage.

When the animation occurs separately from the live action, the negative is cut into the original. If animation has been superimposed over live action, the two are combined in the optical printer, giving you an optical negative. In long productions, this is cut into your original; in shorter productions, it becomes your original.

Opticals and animation, then, are expensive but necessary post production activities. The charge will include layout time, artwork, and footage charges for effects. If you are using computerized animation, such as the HS 200 in tape or the counterpart in film, the charges are hourly, not per effect. It is best, when preparing your estimate, to get the advice of a professional optical house and-or animation house. There is no charge for this service and it will help you prepare a more accurate budget.

The following price quotations are typical for optical effect and animation work:

OPTICAL EFFECTS

16mm and 35mm

	Color	per ft.	B & W	per ft.
Scene fades	4.00		3.00	
Scene dissolve	8.00		6.00	
Focus effect	37.50	6.50	30.00	6.00
Blowup of scene	16.00		12.00	
Reduction of scene	16.00		12.00	
Repositioning of scene	16.00		12.00	
Skip frame	12.00	1.00	8.00	1.00
Double frame	12.00	1.00	8.00	1.00
Reverse angle	16.00		12.00	
Reverse action	12.00		8.00	
Freeze frame	10.00		8.00	
Double exposure	30.00	1.00	25.00	.75
Spin scene freeze frame	70.00	6.50	55.00	6.00
Straighten or tilt scene	37.50	6.50	30.00	6.00
Push across each side	35.00		30.00	
Ripple effect	37.50	6.50	30.00	6.00
Color title	32.00	2.00		
Color title with drop shadow	45.00	3.00		
Title with drop shadow over live	25.00	1.50	20.00	1.00
Additional title run	5.00		5.00	
Burn in only, over live	20.00	1.00	15.00	.75
Insert over live	55.00	2.00	35.00	1.50
Additional matte runs	20.00	1.00	20.00	1.00
Split screen, 2-way	55.00	2.00	45.00	1.50
Split screen, 3-way	75.00	3.00	65.00	2.50
Split screen, 4-way	95.00	4.00	85.00	3.50
Two-way invisible split screen	85.00	3.50	70.00	3.50
Scene wipe	14.00		9.00	
Scene flip	28.00		20.00	
Bi-pack run	20.00	1.00	15.00	.75

Optical Layout Time $10 per hour

	Color	per ft.	B & W	per ft.
Straight zoom	35.00	7.00	30.00	6.00
Zoom and pan	45.00	8.00	35.00	7.00
Pan	35.00	7.00	30.00	6.00

					Minimum Charge	
	Color	per ft	B & W	per ft.	Color	B & W
Optical Negative	.60		30		30.00	25.00
Reversal dupe	.75				40.00	
Precision fine grain			.21			20.00
Precision pan master			.21			20.00
Precision interpositive	.50				25.00	
Precision high contrast			.21			20.00
35mm check prints from optical negative	.17		.10		15.00	10.00
Optical print	.35		.20		30.00	25.00
Cord-to-cord duping add'l	.10		.10			
Cinex (per scene)	2.00		1.00		20.00	10.00

16 to 35 blowup footage	.65	40	30.00	30.00
35 to 16 reduction footage	.65	.40	35.00	30.00
16 to 16	.65	.40	35.00	30.00
16mm A&B duping (add'l)	.10	.10	10.00	10.00
16mm check print from optical negative	.17	.17	17.00	17.00
16mm check print from Ektachrome	.20			20.00
Liquid gate add'l	.05			
Squeezing or unsqueezing	.80	.60	50.00	50.00
Scanning			30.00	30.00
Cinemascope setup			30.00	30.00

ANIMATION STAND PHOTOGRAPHY
(per foot)

	35mm	16mm	Minimum
Color photography	.60	.65	35.00
Black-and-white photography	.45	.50	30.00
Matte & title photography (with high-contrast print)	.55	.60	35.00

ANIMATION STAND EFFECTS
16mm and 35mm B & W

		Minimum
Fades	2.50	
Dissolves	5.00	
Wipes	10.00	
Zooms	6.00 per ft.	30.00
Zooms & pans	7.00 per ft.	35.00
Pans	6.00 per ft.	30.00
Spins & pans	7.00 per ft.	35.00
Out of focus	4.00 per ft.	35.00
Title position	10.00	

16mm and 35mm Color

		Minimum
Fades	4.00	
Dissolves	8.00	
Wipes	15.00	
Zooms	7.00 per ft.	35.00
Zooms & pans	8.00 per ft.	45.00
Pans	7.00 per ft.	35.00
Spins & pans	8.00 per ft.	40.00
Out of focus	5.00 per ft.	40.00
Title position	15.00	

All footage units based on 16mm frames per ft. (35mm)

Courtesy of Coastal Film Service Co.

Chapter 14

Miscellaneous

In every production there are certain expense items that do not fit into any specific category. Such things as production insurance, animal rentals, special clothing, story rights, writer's fees, etc., are sometimes needed. When preparing your estimate from a script or storyboard, always watch for the different or unusual. For example, if a high circling shot is indicated, how will it be achieved? Will you need to rent a helicopter or airplane with a Tyler mount (support for the camera)? Are you shooting underwater? Will you need skindiving equipment, scuba gear, underwater housings for the cameras, etc.? Will there be special writer's fees? Is it an original concept or will you have to pay for story rights or royalties?

WRITER'S FEES

Writer's fees, for the sake of this discussion, are considered below-the-line costs (see Chapter 1 for definition). In major networks and large studios, these are considered above-the-line, as is all talent. Since that varies, though, with each company, we will consider it a below-the-line cost. Writer's fees can range from $100 to $100,000, depending on what has been negotiated. If you are preparing a preliminary budget and have not negotiated a fee with a writer and want to know how much to put into the budget, call the local Writer's Guild and ask them what the scale payment is for your project. Most writers work as independent contractors, so there is no need to include payroll taxes. As with the other trade unions, include pension and welfare contributions in your estimate.

Is your production the adaptation of an existing story or concept? If so, you may have to pay a flat fee to the original author for the right to use it. Or, the original author may ask for a small royalty if there are to be a number of sales or rentals. Be sure, if the storyline is not original, to get the proper clearance and releases from the author. A little money spent on story rights will save a lot of money in legal fees and lawsuits if production is begun without author approval.

ANIMAL RENTALS

Sometimes a script or storyboard calls for the use of an animal. If it is not necessary to have a highly trained one and it is a common house animal, such as a cat or dog, use a friend's. This way your expense will be minimal. However, if the animal must perform or is out of the ordinary, you will need to rent one. There are companies, particularly in the major east and west coast markets, who handly only animals for film and video tape productions. These animals are rented to the production. The figures to be included in your estimate will be for the animal plus the accompanying trainer. The price charged will be determined by the animal, what he must do, how long he must work, etc. Also, if the animal must be transported any distance, you must pay for the transportation of the animal as well as that of his trainer. In addition, they both receive travel pay and all expenses (food and lodging). Some animal rental companies even insist on special insurance coverage. Because of the many variances in usage and time involved, as well as the varieties of animals, there is no basic rate card for animal rentals. When putting a budget together where animals are involved, call one of the rental agencies to determine what prices should be included in your estimate.

If the needed animal is not readily available in your production area, consider the possibility of taking your production to the animal. It might be cheaper and-or easier by the time you consider transportation and all expenses for the trainer and animal, plus rehearsal and shooting days. As of this writing, there are no trained large cats (i.e., lions, cougars, etc.) available on the east coast; you can get them only on the west coast.

SPECIAL EFFECTS

Does your production call for any unusual shots that cannot be achieved optically or by special effects, such as an underwater shot or a high circling one? If so, include the necessary equipment and supplies to make the shot possible. If it is being done underwater, allow for underwater housings for the cameras, scuba equipment and-or underwater platforms or cages for the cameramen. Also allow for boat rentals to get you to the location designated for the underwater shooting.

Allow for boat rentals, too, if you are doing any shooting on the water, such as sailboat races, a moonlight boat ride, motorboat rallies, etc. This includes the boats for your crews and-or boats as props in the scene to be shot. These are rented by the hour, day, or longer, if needed.

When your production has a high aerial shot or a low flying one, include airplane or helicopter rentals in your estimate as well as a Tyler mount for the camera. The airplane is either rented by the hour, day, or week, depending on your needs, and the Tyler mount by the day.

INSURANCE

No production should begin without proper insurance coverage. Usually, this amount averages 2 to 3 percent of your total below-the-line budget. It is possible, when doing a large volume of production business, to get a "dice" blanket policy. This is an all-inclusive policy that can be purchased at a lower rate due to production volume. For example, if your below-the-line production costs in any one year are at least $500,000, your rate could be as low as 1½ percent. This insurance is available through any registered agent. The only two types of insurance not covered under this all-inclusive policy are Workmen's Compensation and Comprehensive General Liability. They are separate policies.

Depending on what you are shooting and the type of production, you should carry some or all of the following types of insurance.

1. **Workmen's compensation** is required by law and provides coverage for any injury that is sustained as a direct result of an occupation. The benefits are provided under individual state laws, with several states having "monopolistic systems," whereby insurance must be placed with a local governmental representative. The benefits of this policy are usually limited to medical expense reimbursement and-or loss of time. The rate for this insurance varies with the number of employees and the number of working days. On foreign productions, coverage must comply with the individual country's requirements. A "voluntary compensation rider" can be included on the policy that makes the benefits comparable to the state of hire for citizens of the United States.

2. **Comprehensive general-auto liability** is one of the most important policies that any producer can have. This protects

the producer against any legal action as a result of bodily injury or property damage. A basic policy provides limits of $100,000 per person, a total policy coverage of $300,000 and property damage liability in the amount of $50,000. The charge for this is a flat premium, billed yearly, and is not based on the amount or volume of production. The current price is $350 per year. This can be supplemented by an Excess Catastrophe Umbrella Policy, giving additional coverage of $1,000,000 or more, over and above the basic coverage. It is not recommended for the average production. This policy should also provide coverage for "auto nonownership liability" covering all automobiles that are rented, loaned, or donated to the production. Liability insurance should also include coverage of the people working as independent contractors.

3. **Negative insurance,** sometimes referred to as "All-Risk Negative" insurance, pays for the cost of reshooting any phase of your production that is lost or damaged as a result of malfunctioning equipment, faulty lab work, or faulty raw stock. Negative insurance includes coverage on raw stock, positives, workprints, fine-grain prints, sound tracks, and tape used in connection with a production. The insurance is billed two separate ways. The higher rate is used through the period of time that you are editing, up to delivery of the final answer print. The storage rate is maintained after delivery and approval of the answer print until such time as the negative is no longer needed or being used. The storage rate is appreciably lower than the production rate.

4. **Equipment insurance**: Miscellaneous equipment coverage can be issued to provide coverage on a specific list of equipment, or on a blanket form providing coverage on all owned and rented equipment. The policy provides coverage not only on cameras and camera equipment, but sound and lighting equipment, electrical equipment, mechanical effects equipment, hand props, and grip equipment.

5. **Props, sets, and wardrobe**: This section of a policy provides coverage for any loss or damage to scenery, costumes, theatrical property and wardrobe.

6. **Extra expense insurance** is referred to as "all risks of direct physical loss or damage" coverage and protects the producer against any loss incurred as a result of an interruption, postponement or cancellation of a scheduled shooting day or production that is a **direct result** of the damage to or destruction of property or facilities being used for the production. When obtaining this insurance, be sure the agent spells out the many qualifications and exclusions that limit the coverage.

7. **Third-party property damage:** Under this policy the insurance company agrees to pay for damage to anything that the producer is **legally obligated** to pay as a result of damage or destruction to the property of others. For example, any rental equipment that is damaged or stolen would be protected under this policy. As with extra expense insurance, there are limitations to the coverage, so be sure to find out what they are before production begins.

8. **Cast insurance:** Normally, this applies only to feature film production and coverage is limited to the director, key members of the cast, and, on occasion, the cameraman. For example, if halfway through a production the leading man is injured, dies, or becomes ill and cannot continue with the production, all the costs incurred as a result of either stopping the production or having to start all over again will be paid by the insurance company.

9. **Errors and omissions insurance** is particularly important coverage for cinema verite' productions, since many times you are not able to get signed releases from all the people who are recognizable on camera. This insurance protects you "for any claim made or commenced against a producer or distributor of a film for libel, slander, defamation of character, invasion of privacy, infringement of copyright, whether under statutory or common law, breach of implied contract in connection with the alleged submission of any literary or musical material, or unauthorized use of titles, formats, ideas, characters, plots, or other program material. This policy does not include coverage for punitive damages."

10. **Accident insurance:** A special group accident policy has been worked out for motion picture production companies, including coverage for aerial photography, stunt photography, and other risks as required. The standard policy provides world-wide coverage on each person in the amount of $100,000 for accidental death and dismemberment, blanket medical expense reimbursement in the amount of $2,500 with no deductible amount, and indemnity in the amount of $150 per week or more for a period of one year. This can be supplemented as required by additional insurance.

11. **Weather insurance:** Usually, this is written only for location shooting and the standard policy covers rain only. Sometimes, however, this can be expanded to cover any adverse weather that might affect your production. This insurance pays for all expenses incurred as a result of bad weather interrupting your shooting schedule. For example, camera rentals, payments to crews, and prop rentals—monies that must be paid even if production is halted for the day. This

insurance would **not** cover any payments that could be cancelled or deferred.

Insurance items 3 through 11 listed above are all part of the 2 to 3 percent of your total production budget that you should include under insurance.

What else is considered miscellaneous? There isn't enough room for all the exceptions. However, if it's a cost area and cannot be fitted into your budget under a definite category, it belongs under "miscellaneous."

Chapter 15
Overhead

Overhead in a production budget refers to the percentage or amount of your operating expenses that are applicable to the production. In a large production house or facility, these figures are not listed separately, but, instead, are either part of the markup (profit) or are included in the basic equipment rental prices, lab charges, etc. A producer who has no facilities but relies totally on suppliers cannot "hide" these overhead figures as easily as a large producer. Therefore, it is recommended that they be handled in the following manner.

There are five main categories to be considered: 1) space, 2) telephone charges, 3) messenger services, 4) office supplies and 5) administrative and office personnel.

SPACE

What percentage of your staff's time will be spent on the production you are budgeting? How many weeks or months do you think will be needed to take the production from the planning stages through to finished product? For example, if the production will take approximately 40 percent of your time for six months, take 40 percent of your monthly office rent (including electricity and heat if applicable) and multiply it by six months for the figure to be entered in "space" (Fig. 15-1). If you work out of your home, the decision is yours as to whether or not there should be any amount listed in this area. If the budget is tight, this is one section where the figures can be trimmed and-or eliminated.

TELEPHONE

Telephone expenses can vary greatly from job to job. If you are located in New York and your production is in California, the budgeted figures will be much greater than, say, if you are located in New York and working in New York. Will you need to install additional lines and-or phones for the

```
$   720.00  #1 "Space" ... $300 a month X .40 X 6 months

    360.00  #2 "Telephone" ... $15/week X 24 weeks

    600.00  #3 "Messengers" ... $25/week X 24 weeks

    300.00  #4 "Supplies" ... $50/month X 6 months

  6,585.60  #5 "Office Personnel"

                a.  Bookkeeper @ $175/week X .40 X 24 weeks

                b.  Production Secretary @ $200/week X .50 X 24 weeks

                c.  Purchasing Clerk @ $150/week X .50 X 24 weeks

                d.  12% of the above for payroll taxes

$8,565.60  TOTAL
```

Fig. 15-1. Sample overhead budget.

duration of the production? If so, include the installation charges, monthly billings, and message unit charges in addition to the estimated long-distance figures. On overseas production, be particularly careful in this area. Budget sufficient money to allow for any and all calls that might have to be made overseas. As a starting point, a good rule of thumb for an average local production is to allow $15 a week for telephone charges from the very beginning of production planning through to completion.

MESSENGER SERVICES

How will the film get to and from the labs; who will pick up and deliver equipment; what about daily deliveries to the client? If you have someone on the staff who will be handling these various errands for you, allot a percentage of their salary to the section on "messengers." If you run the errands yourself, you may not wish to enter any figure here but, instead, have this be part of your service as producer. If you will be using outside services, figure out an average number of weekly runs, the charges for these runs, and include that figure in the budget. If the pickups are large and will involve a truck or car or even motorcycle, be sure to include those charges. In New York, where the average charge per errand is $2.50, 10 trips a week cost $25. To start with, use $25 a week as an average amount for the entire production time.

OFFICE SUPPLIES

"Supplies" on the budget form include not only paper,

143

stationary, etc., but also postage. Are there scripts to be typed? Will there be revisions and how many? Will there be considerable mailings to the client? Although there can be great variations from production to production, a basic amount to use is $50 a month.

ADMINISTRATIVE & OFFICE PERSONNEL

"Office personnel" refers to bookkeeper(s), production secretary(s), and purchasing clerk(s). How many people are on your staff and what percentage of their time will be spent on the production you are budgeting? If a secretary, purchasing clerk, and-or bookkeeper are hired specifically for the production, allot their full salary for the time they will be employed by the production, plus 12 percent payroll taxes. If, on the other hand, you already have a staff that consists of these people, estimate what percentage of their time they will be involved in this production and put that figure in the budget. For example, as shown in the sample budget, this production would take 40 percent of a bookkeeper's time and 50 percent each of a production secretary and purchasing clerk's time. Take the percentage of time they are involved and multiply this figure by their weekly salary and the total number of weeks of the production from preplanning through to completion. Unless you are hiring these people as independent contractors, just for the duration of the production, remember to add 12 percent of the total salaries for payroll taxes. This 12 percent covers unemployment insurance, disability insurance, and employer's equal FICA contribution.

Although it is to your advantage to break out these figures in your estimate, you can "guesstimate" by just taking 10 percent of your overall below-the-line budget, calling it "general and administrative," and adding it to the total budget. This is not as accurate as itemizing each category, but if you are rushed and need to prepare a fast estimate, 10 percent is a logical percentage to use.

Chapter 16

Nonunion Production

Many production estimates are based on using union personnel and union wage scales with the applicable pension and welfare contributions to the various unions included. Not all productions, however, use union personnel. These nonunion budgets are much simpler to prepare, since you do not have to know all the union rules, regulations, and contingent cost factors to prepare an accurate estimate. As contrasted to union productions, there are no set rules for nonunion shooting. The following guidelines will show the similarities and differences in each cost area.

What are some of the factors that make you decide to shoot nonunion? Of prime importance can be budgetary limitations. Are you restricted to a certain amount of money? Since there are fewer job categories on a nonunion production, the total cost can be cut by as much as 40 percent. How mobile must you be? The fewer people on your production, the more flexible you can be, and with flexibility comes creativity. With a nonunion production, you have a minimum crew and are, therefore, more mobile. What is your completion time? If you have a short period of time to finish your project, the chances of completing it by your deadline are better with nonunion personnel than union, since they often work for flat rates and are willing to work longer hours to finish up a project in a shorter period of time.

Although nonunion production is more prevalent in film than video tape, it is not uncommon to find nonunion production in video tape, too. If you are planning on doing a video tape production, nonunion, keep in mind that you must have technicians who are familiar with the equipment and know how to handle it. Also remember that since handheld cameras and mobile tape equipment are still in the experimental and testing stages (as of this writing), they are still too cumbersome to compete with film on the same level. In the majority of cases, video tape technicians are union personnel (except in areas where all the technicians are nonunion). Therefore, it is not feasible, at this writing, to devote much time to nonunion video tape production, since it has not reached the same level of sophistication as nonunion film production.

The following are the budget areas involved in both union and nonunion production with specifics as to the similarities and differences between the two types of production.

The budget categories in which there are no differences are as follows:

Studios and locations: The rates are the same for a nonunion production as for one that is union.

Raw stock: The charges for film stock, audio tape, and video tape are the same for all productions.

Laboratory charges: These rates, too, are not determined by the type of production but merely by what is sent to the lab.

Transfer charges: The same applies here as to lab charges.

Post production (opticals, mixing, music, animation, sound effects): These, too, are not affected by the use of union or nonunion personnel. They are separate subentities and are computed on a different basis than the actual production itself.

One of the major areas in which there is no difference is talent. Whether or not your production is sanctioned by the union should have no effect on the talent or method of payment. Always pay talent the applicable SAG or AFTRA scale. As contrasted to production and technical personnel, there are few, if any, talented nonunion performers. When preparing a nonunion budget, as with one for a union production, the following should be included in your talent estimate. If SAG, use the rates as dictated by the code books, plus pension and welfare contributions to the union and 12 percent payroll taxes. If your bid is based on the AFTRA scale, use the applicable rates plus 10 percent agent's fees, the necessary pension and welfare contributions to the union, and 12 percent payroll taxes. You will notice that the only **major** difference between the two talent unions is the payment of the agent's fee. However, this can add greatly to your overall budget if you have a large cast, and it should be considered when preparing the budget (see Chapter 8).

The following budget categories reflect some differences between union and nonunion production and the variables are pointed out.

OVERHEAD

As was discussed in Chapter 15, this figure is sometimes included in the fee to the production facility or in the markup. However, if you are an independent producer and break out the figures in this category, your total budget cost is more realistic. It is possible, with a nonunion production, for this part of your budget to be slightly lower than that of a union production, since the bookkeeping will be simpler and in all probability the production time will be shorter. Because of this shorter production schedule, the need for office space, secretarial fees, telephone charges, and supplies is not as extensive as in a union production.

SURVEY

A survey that is not in your immediate vicinity can be quite costly for a union production. Not only are you required to pay union wages, but you must also pay for travel time, per diem, transportation (first class), union pension and welfare contributions, and payroll taxes. In a nonunion production this figure can be cut dramatically if you have neogtiated flat fees with the various production and technical personnel you are using. If a survey is included in their total package price to you, the only figures that will have to be included in this area for a nonunion budget are the transportation charges for those surveying the production area, car rental if necessary, food, and lodging.

EQUIPMENT

Although most equipment prices are standard for both union and nonunion productions, there will be some savings in this area. First, you will not need as much equipment as in a union production because you will have fewer production personnel. Also, in nonunion productions, as in union productions, many cameramen and soundmen have their own equipment and prefer to use it and rent it to the production at a reduced rate rather than getting equipment from an official rental house such as F&B Ceco or Camera Mart. This not only cuts down on problems due to equipment failure but also eliminates the need for an additional day of equipment rental for testing purposes.

SCENIC ELEMENTS

Usually, nonunion is synonomous with cinema verite and, therefore, is shot at actual locations rather than on fabricated sets. However, if sets are to be designed, there are three areas where you will definitely save money on a nonunion production. First, small hand props can be picked up by a production secretary or production assistant rather than a union outside prop man. Second, if large props such as furniture, sets, etc., must be picked up, you do not have to use union truckers but can, instead, use someone on the production staff. (Unless, of course, the pickup is from a union shop. Then you have no choice but to use the teamsters.) Third, if the floor has to be painted in the studio, you do not have to have members of the Scenic Artists Union do it but can hire outside people.

LOCATION EXPENSES

Since there are no set rules for per diem, travel time, first-class accommodations, etc., as there are in union productions, you can realize considerable savings in this area on a nonunion production. Travel expenses are cut down because there are fewer people involved in the production. As was discussed in Chapter 10, all the unions have a set per diem figure as well as specific rules and regulations on plane reservations, hotel-motel accommodations, and food allowance. On a nonunion production, a realistic per diem figure to use is $35 per man per 24 hour day. This breaks down to $20 a day for lodging and $15 a day for food. Taxis, gratuities, telephone, and laundry charges are in addition to this.

If your crew is going to be on location for an extended period of time (one month or longer) you can save money in lodging expenses by renting a house or apartment rather than having them stay in a hotel for the entire time. You can also cut down on location expenses by confining your production to a reasonable radius of your home base. In this way your crew can return home each night and you save on food and lodging. This, of course, depends on your script. Don't sacrifice creativity for monetary reasons.

EDITING

Since there are no union rules to consider, you usually do not need an assistant editor, unless the show itself demands one. You can make an agreement with your editor for a flat fee for the production rather than paying union scale with attendant overtime, pension and welfare, and payroll taxes. Also, if you pay the editor as an independent contractor, not only do you save the 12 percent in payroll taxes, but you also are not involved in the many government tax reports that can be both confusing and time consuming. The other cost factors—negative cutting, equipment rental, supplies, etc.—are about the same as outlined in Chapter 12.

TECHNICAL AND PRODUCTION PERSONNEL

This is the area of biggest savings in a nonunion production. Here you are not restricted to specific starting and stopping times, legal holidays, double time, golden time, short turnaround, etc. (see Chapter 7). There are no specific crew requirements; i.e., for each cameraman there must be an assistant, for each soundman an assistant, etc. Your production may be such that you might need these people, but with a nonunion production you have the freedom to decide rather than being obligated to carry a certain number of men on your production.

When hiring your crew, use the union rates as a point of reference. There are many cameramen and soundmen who prefer to work for flat daily rates rather than 8-hour days with overtime, etc., and there are many production personnel who will also work this way. Oftentimes, these are people who make more than the union scale but, because of their artistic ability and their contribution to the production, can demand more money. And, even though they make more than the union sets as a minimum, you will still save money because they often work as independent contractors and, therefore, no payroll taxes need to be paid. Since it is not a union production, pension and welfare contributions and all the reports that go with it are not required.

As was mentioned earlier, much nonunion production is cinema verité. Since it is shot "as it happens," you can eliminate many of your production personnel such as hairdressers, make-up artists, wardrobe handlers, etc. Again, if your production calls for these people, try to negotiate a flat rate and have them work as independent contractors rather than paying them through a payroll.

Please notice that on a nonunion production, there are better opportunities to make more money as a cameraman, soundman, or even production assistant because there are fewer people on the crew and no set rules, and, therefore, more flexibility in negotiating a salary. Nonunion is not synonomous with low pay or cheap production. Although it can be more economical, it is not necessarily "bargain basement."

Although there are no restrictions for getting a nonunion production on television, there are some for theatre showings. A union seal does not need to appear on television, but does need to be on a theatrical release. If your production is done with nonunion personnel, it may be necessary to purchase a union seal before you can release your film.

Where do you find nonunion personnel? If you are a novice or beginner, it's almost impossible to know where to start. As contrasted to a union production, where you can call the union for suggestions, there is no centralized referral agency for nonunion personnel. The only way you find these people is through experience, friends, and watching the credits on nonunion productions. As you gain experience, your list of available nonunion personnel grows.

Chapter 17
Sample Budgets

There are as many ways of budgeting as there are budgets. The sample estimates included here cover a variety of productions from a 30-second video tape commercial to an hour-long film documentary to a 35mm feature film. Each production was estimated on different forms with different rates. You will notice, though, the consistency of the general categories.

The first budget is for two 60-second commercials done in color, on video tape, in New York City. This is a very brief form with a minimum of itemization and a number of questions left unanswered. You will notice there is no breakdown of what equipment is being used or how many personnel or, for that matter, even what personnel. This is the type of budget that is submitted to a client as a bid for a particular job without any listing of details. In this price the producer has included a markup for profit as well as any administrative and overhead expenses he may incur. These figures probably reflect a 40 percent markup on actual costs.

SAMPLE 1: Two 60-second commercials, color, videotape

Day 1

Camera and VTR production unit (10 hours)	$2000.00
Two hours overtime at $200 per hour	400.00
Insert stage (10 hours)	325.00
Two hours overtime at $25 per hour (stage)	50.00
Video tape stock rental: three reels at $30 per reel	90.00

Day 2

Camera and VTR production unit (10 hours)	1900.00
2½ hours overtime at $200 per hour	500.00
Insert stage (10 hours)	325.00
2½ hours overtime at $25 per hour (stage)	62.50
Video tape stock rental, four reels at $30 per reel	120.00
One master tape at $20	20.00
Switcher	150.00
VR2000 for playback: 9 hours at $100 per hour	900.00
One protection master	35.00

Subtotal	$6877.50

Pre-edit after Day 1 shoot

Two hours, three VTRs at $300 per hour	600.00
Stock for pre-edit	20.00
Editorial: 6 hours, two VTRs at $200 per hour	1200.00

Total, production and editorial:	$8697.50

In contrast, here is a video tape budget for two commercials, a 30-second spot with a 20-second lift, shot in color in New York. You will notice that this estimate lists the equipment, personnel, number of hours involved and, in general, all production details. As a point of comparison, the actual costs of the production are listed adjacent to the estimated amounts. As you can see by comparing the total production costs, this estimate was quite accurate. An experienced estimator will prepare an accurate budget that is fairly close to the actual costs of the production.

SAMPLE 2: One 30-second commercial, one 20-second lift, color, video tape

	Estimated	Actual
Equipment rental (1 camera, 2 VTRs)	827.00	$827.00

1 hour with 2 cameras, no second cameraman	164.00	164.00
Camera lens	---	15.60
1 crab dolly	65.00	45.00
Video tape: 2 hours rental, 2 hours purchase	510.00	390.00
Personnel: 1 TD, 1 audio man, 1 tape man, 1 cameraman, 1 video man, 1 utility man (15 hours including travel time and 2 meal penalties)	907.00	1,099.00
Director	750.00	450.00
Associate director	70.00	126.21
Stage manager	63.00	115.34
Production supervisor	100.00	100.00
Make-up	65.00	65.00
Hairdresser	65.00	174.80
Wardrobe	50.00	139.75
Talent: 2 on camera with 3 hours overtime and 1 Extra	579.00	906.00
Overtime for AD, SM, PS, MU, hair, wardrobe	336.00	---
Dog	200.00	200.00
Casting	100.00	100.00
Lighting director	200.00	125.00
Three stagehands	336.00	576.00
Equipment, lighting	300.00	---
Trucking of lighting equipment	100.00	---

Location expenses (within 25 miles NYC):

Transportation	---	30.00
Per diem (lunch only)	300.00	---
Travel time (production personnel and talent)	142.00	---
Permits	25.00	---
Survey (TD, LD, producer)	197.00	456.40
Location fees	350.00	500.00

Scenic elements:

Set design	150.00	---
Construction	---	34.50

Props	150.00	173.72
Graphics	100.00	30.00
Costume design, costumes	425.00	500.58
Trucking	150.00	---
Miscellaneous supplies	150.00	12.15

Post production:

Editing: 3 VTRs for 12 hours	1,116.00	837.00
1 VTR, 1 hour for titles	35.00	---
Pre-record, 1 hour	50.00	50.00
Audio mix, 1½ hours	165.00	110.00
Post production personnel	150.00	100.00
Video tape for post production	30.00	56.88
Sound effects	50.00	---
Viewing time	---	7.75
Miscellaneous	200.00	175.00
Total out-of-pocket costs	$ 9,722.00	$8,692.68
Overhead-profit	4,180.00	3,737.85
Production total	$13,902.00	$12,430.53

The client was quoted $13,000 to do this job.

Here's another video tape budget, this time poorly estimated. It's for three commercials: one 75 seconds, one 60 seconds, and one 30 seconds. Again, shot in color in New York. The overages in this estimate occurred in the scenic elements section, in the area of stagehands, and in editing. In reading through the producer's notes after completion of the project, it was noted that some of the production requirements were not mentioned at the time of bidding. A good producer clearly states what various items are covered by his budget and anything over and above that is a billable extra. Again, as with Sample 2, both estimated and actual cost figures are given for comparison.

SAMPLE 3: One 75-, one 60-, one 30-second commercial, color, video tape.

	Estimated	Actual
Rental, 2 cameras, 2 VTRs	$2,310.00	$1,982.00
Rental, 1 camera, 2 VTRs	788.00	---
1 Chapman crane	466.00	325.00
Video tape stock, 3 hours purchase, 3 hours rental	760.00	449.00
Prism	---	25.00
Eight technicians	1,430.00	1,697.00

Production personnel:

	Estimated	Actual
Director	600.00	600.00
Associate director	166.00	226.00
Stage manager	150.00	192.00
Production supervisor	250.00	200.00
Overscale, hairdresser	200.00	---
Overscale, make-up	100.00	65.00
Lighting director	525.00	450.00
Stagehands	1,444.00	2,902.00
Lighting equipment	750.00	1,179.00
Trucking, lighting equipment	100.00	100.00

Location expenses:

	Estimated	Actual
Permit	25.00	25.00

Scenic elements:

	Estimated	Actual
Set design	900.00	---
Scenic artist	250.00	1,037.00
Construction	2,000.00	3,674.00
Props	500.00	112.00
Graphics	30.00	742.00
Trucking	300.00	218.00
*Security guard (72 hours)	---	308.00
Supplies	150.00	---
Studio rental	2,134.00	3,813.00
*Signs on set	---	214.00

Post production:

	Estimated	Actual
**Editing, 3 VTRs, 14 hours	1,302.00	2,464.00
Photoscripts	---	15.00

Prerecord	100.00	181.00
Film transfer, 1 hour	62.00	8.00
Audio mix, 2 hours	220.00	289.00
Technicolor kine	---	110.00
Three prints of each commercial	---	630.00
Editing personnel	100.00	100.00
Video tape for editing	75.00	150.00
35mm hot kines (3 spots)	---	213.00
Still photographer	---	101.00
Miscellaneous	200.00	294.00
Total out-of-pocket costs	$18,287.00	$25,090.00
Overhead-profit	7,863.00	10,036.00
Production total	$26,150.00	$35,126.00

Price quoted to the client was
$24,600.

* This was a closed set for a secret product. Therefore, a guard and signs were needed so that unauthorized personnel were not allowed in the studio or control room.
** Editing ran 26½ hours

This next budget is a simple one for an hour-long documentary, shot in 16mm, color. The producers of this program were restricted to $50,000 for the program and stayed well within that figure. Notice that 50 percent of the budget was spent for salaries (camera crew and film editing staff); 10 percent for raw stock and lab costs. These are high percentages for a budget of this amount. Notice, too, the small amount of money spent for equipment rentals. Since the cameramen were hired with their own equipment, some of these charges are included in the salary figures. This explains the high percentage for salaries.

In addition, there is no money listed as being spent for editing equipment or supplies. This, too, is included in the $15,000 figure for editing staff salaries. One of the major criticisms of this budget is its lack of details; there are too many questions left unanswered.

SAMPLE 4: One-hour documentary, 16mm film

Talent	$1,150.00
Staff travel (including car rentals)	1,637.72
Staff per diem (including hotel, taxis, etc.)	3,271.30
Talent travel	56.00
Camera crew salary (including payroll taxes)	10,008.79
Camera crew travel (including car rentals)	1,064.06
Camera equipment rental	115.00
Lighting equipment rental (field)	8.00
Raw stock	2,613.60
Raw stock processing	8,408.97
Mix	1,691.81
Sound transfers	100.00
Transcription typing of interviews	654.95
¼-inch tape	96.30
16mm magnetic tape	1,620.50
Film editing staff salaries	15,000.00
Graphics and titles	1,530.87
Music and sound effects	60.00
Screenings	107.00
Insurance, taxes	50.62
Messenger service (film shipments from shoots)	90.14
Research materials (in field)	83.45
Total	**$49,989.55**

The following budget is for a 90-minute show, presented five times a week. These costs are for all five shows, color, New York, video tape. As with Sample 4, there are too many summarized figures, leaving many questions as to what has been included and what has been left out.

SAMPLE 5: Five 90-minute shows, color, video tape

Regular talent	$8,619.00
Extra musicians	833.00
Orchestra, including leader	8,060.00
Ticket office and manpower	750.00
Engineering and equipment	10,074.00
Stagehands	4,908.00
Scenic designer, scenic artist, make-up, wardrobe, stage manager	1,825.00

Production staff:

Producor, director, assistant director, talent coordinators, associate producers	6,305.00
Writers	3,250.00
Video tape costs, original copies	1,265.00
Tape costs for distribution	1,755.00
Dubbing, VTRs, material, manpower	1,686.00
Staff salaries, dubbing center	600.00
Star base pay	8,000.00
Storage, trucking, new sets, cleaning, miscellaneous	625.00
Total	$58,555.00

The above total does not include the following:

1. Allocation of the business manager's and his assistant's salary and related costs.
2. Allocation of the salaries of the production president, executive vice president or production supervisor of the company sponsoring this program.
3. Allocation of personnel from advertising, press relations, sales, business office, and other staff. In other words, no allocation of any overhead payroll expenses.
4. Production company pension and welfare payments.
5. Miscellaneous expense allowances to the production staff (lunches, etc.).
6. Allocation of depreciation expense on equipment owned by the production company in the dubbing center.
7. General overhead: rent, telephone, etc.

The next two budgets are excellent. All categories are listed and broken down into detail. There are very few questions left unanswered. Both of these estimates are for hour-long, cinema verite' documentaries shot in 16mm color. As with Samples 2 and 3, the actual costs are listed right next to the budgeted amounts. As you will notice, the 15 percent contingency was important on both of them because it gave the producer a "cushion" against overages. A note here about a contingency. Always add at least 10 percent of the total production price to your estimate to cover any unexpected overages or problems. If you complete your production without using the contingency, it can either be additional profit to you or, if you wish, you can rebate it to your client. **Always include a contingency.**

SAMPLE 6: One-hour documentary, 16mm color

	Estimated	Actual
Overhead:		
Space	$ ---	---
Telephone	500.00	627.29
Messengers	250.00	146.50
Supplies	150.00	67.18
Miscellaneous	500.00	750.16
Production personnel:		
Producer	16,000.00	16,000.00
Director	5,000.00	5,000.00
Writer	1,500.00	1,500.00
Associate producer	5,975.00	6,000.00
Cameramen	7,005.00	7,280.50
Asst. cameramen	3,075.00	2,857.10
Soundmen	2,380.00	1,087.00
Electricians	---	---
Unit manager	---	---
Production assistant	1,750.00	1,282.00
Location expenses:		
Food	2,475.00	3,262.47
Lodging	3,241.00	3,487.10
Travel	3,482.00	4,789.53
Car rentals	1,710.00	2,548.09
Shipping	1,940.00	659.84
Gratuities	400.00	643.84
Releases	100.00	50.00
Miscellaneous	895.00	2,975.51
Equipment:		
Camera-sound	$10,905.00	$13,788.57
Lighting-grip	150.00	18.76
Special-miscellaneous	2,100.00	1,030.50

Stock footage:

Rights	5,000.00	9,525.00
Footage	500.00	704.65

Raw stock:

Film	4,415.00	5,830.78
Tape	420.00	256.56

Laboratory:

Developing	4,337.00	5,027.24
Workprinting	6,321.00	5,554.59
Slop prints	160.00	107.21
Coding	778.00	606.60
Miscellaneous	200.00	---

Transfers:

Stock	1,268.00	1,169.49
Time	1,750.00	957.54
Transcriptions	1,205.00	136.47

Editing:

Editor	5,200.00	10,742.50
Assistant editor	2,550.00	4,559.20
Negative cutter	1,000.00	1,060.00
Equipment rentals	1,500.00	4,405.96
Room rental	---	300.00
Supplies	500.00	1,004.38
Miscellaneous	---	

Post production:

Screenings	250.00	390.00
Opticals	550.00	1,156.99
Titles	300.00	1,473.66
Narrator	1,500.00	2,600.00
Recording	200.00	380.00
Music	4,000.00	3,135.23
Pre-mix and mix	1,500.00	1,523.20
Additional tracks	300.00	925.50
Answer print	640.00	313.97

Release print	314.00	245.00
Air print	340.00	53.00
Miscellaneous	---	---

Miscellaneous:

Animation	---	---
Consultants	$2,500.00	$2,000.00
Insurance	1,500.00	1,500.00
Petty cash	350.00	463.31
Taxes, pension & welfare	150.00	1,062.30

Subtotal	$122,381.00	$139.022.31
14 percent contingency	17,457.00	---
Total production costs:	$139,838.00	$139,022.31

SAMPLE   7:   One-hour documentary, 16mm color

Overhead:	Estimated	Actual
Space	---	---
Telephone	800.00	800.13
Messengers	400.00	16.50
Supplies	150.00	54.93
Miscellaneous	150.00	163.97

Production personnel:

Producer-director-writer	12,000.00	12,000.00
Cameramen	8,750.00	11,338.36
Assistant cameramen	4,050.00	5,639.00
Soundmen	4,400.00	6,332.50
Electricians	500.00	377.90
Unit manager	400.00	64.51
Production assistant	4,000.00	5,070.00

Location expenses:

Food	2,760.00	3,461.17
Lodging	4,600.00	2,872.80
Travel	6,846.00	9,107.84
Car rentals	380.00	720.62
Shipping	7,235.00	4,432.18

Gratuities	300.00	1,159.88
Releases	100.00	---
Miscellaneous	500.00	3,345.00

Equipment:

Camera	4,800.00	8,053.96
Sound	600.00	1,444.42
Lighting	460.00	182.37
Grip	---	---
Special and miscellaneous	---	113.16

Stock footage:

Rights	6,700.00	6,700.00
Laboratory	400.00	400.00

Raw stock:

Film	5,194.00	4,411.44
Tape	140.00	178.35

Laboratory:

Developing	3,640.00	3,772.22
Workprinting	5,960.00	4,462.86
Slop prints	160.00	161.80
Coding	800.00	1,094.91
Miscellaneous	200.00	---

Transfers:

Stock	1,250.00	1,771.80
Time	1,750.00	660.20
Transcriptions	1,205.00	691.70

Editing:

Editor	6,300.00	15,508.93
Assistant editor	3,600.00	7,560.54
Negative cutter	1,000.00	1,139.50
Equipment rentals	500.00	1,920.11
Supplies	200.00	972.67

Post production:

Screenings	250.00	284.50
Opticals	600.00	89.86
Titles	300.00	890.19
Narrator	800.00	674.90
Recording	200.00	424.25
Music	200.00	225.00
Pre-mix and mix	1,430.00	1,414.40
Additional tracks	200.00	---
Answer print	640.00	651.48
Release print	314.00	15.80
Air print	340.00	230.69
Miscellaneous	160.00	1,113.60

Miscellaneous:

Animation	400.00	2,853.07
Consultants	---	5,000.00
Insurance	5,200.00	5,175.00
Petty cash	---	---
Pension, welfare & taxes	3,741.00	3,973.10
Subtotal	$117,955.00	$150,174.39
15 percent contingency	17,693.00	
Total production cost	$135,648.00	$150.174.39

As you can see in Sample 7, without the contingency they would have suffered a greater loss than they did. Overages in this estimate occurred in the areas of location expenses, equipment, editing, and production personnel. From the budget it appears that the program took longer to shoot than planned and longer to edit.

The last budget is for a 35mm feature film, shot in color, in and around New York City. Study the amount of detail needed for a budget of this size. Compare this 35mm budget with Sample 7, a 16mm documentary. Notice where the big pricing and cost differences occur.

SAMPLE 8: 35mm feature film

ACCOUNT NUMBER	DESCRIPTION		TOTAL	TOTALS	TOTALS	
1	Story				75,000	00
2	Continuity and Treatment				88,000	00
3	Producer				121,000	00
4	Director				42,000	00
5	Cast				22,596	64
6	Bits				8,328	30
7	Extras				6,937	47
	Sub Total				363,862	41
8	Production Staff Salaries				64,900	05
9	Production Operating Staff				118,891	75
10	Set Designing				6,975	00
11	Set Operation Expenses				38,280	00
12	Cutting - Film - Laboratory				108,265	50
13	Music				11,000	00
14	Sound				9,405	00
15	Transportation - Studio				21,708	00
16	Location				31,100	00
17	Studio Rental					
18	Tests and Retakes				950	00
19	Publicity				12,150	00
20	Miscellaneous					
21	Insurance - Taxes - Licenses and Fees				15,725	00
22	General Overhead				32,650	00
	Sub Total				472,000	90
	Grand Total				835,863	31

Approved _____ Producer

Prepared From _____ 125 _____ Page Script Dated _____

_____ 44 _____ Day Shooting Scheduled at _____ _____ Studio

Director _____
Budget by

_____

ACCOUNT NUMBER	DESCRIPTION	DAYS, WKS, OR QUANTITY	RATE	TOTALS	
I	STORY -				
	A. STORY PURCHASE			75,000	00
	B. TITLE PURCHASE				
	TOTAL STORY			75,000	00
2	CONTINUITY AND TREATMENT				
	A. WRITERS Script			15,000	00
	Treatment			25,000	00
	B. STENOGRAPHER Shooting script			8,000	00
	C. MIMEOGRAPH EXPENSE			1,000	00
	D. RESEARCH EXPENSE /development			39,000	00
	TOTAL CONTINUITY AND TREATMENT			88,000	00
3	PRODUCER				
	A. PRODUCER - Development			46,000	00
	Production			75,000	00
	B. ASST. PRODUCER				
	C. SECRETARIES				
	TOTAL PRODUCER			121,000	00
4	DIRECTOR				
	A. DIRECTOR			42,000	00
	B. SECRETARIES				
	C. PENSION CONTRIBUTIONS				
	TOTAL DIRECTORS			42,000	00

ACCOUNT NUMBER	DESCRIPTION	DAYS, WKS, OR QUANTITY	RATE		TOTALS	
5	CAST Bob	9 wk.	500	00	4,500	00
	Marie	9 wk.	500	00	4,500	00
	Nick	9 wk.	450	00	4,050	00
	Karl	8 wk.	450	00	3,600	00
	Don	4 wk.	450	00	1,800	
	sub total				18,450	00
	Overtime-15% of $18,450.00				2,767	50
	Pension and Welfare -6-1/2% of $21,217.50				1,379	14
	BUYOUTS		128½			
	PENSION H&W CONTRIBUTIONS					
	TOTAL CAST				22,596	64
6	BITS Skid row bum	1 day	120	00	120	00
	Grey Panhandler	1 day	120	00	120	00
	Irish Lady	1 day	120	00	120	00
	Man with pack	1 day	120	00	120	00
	Aunt Mary	2 days	150	00	300	00
	Cycle Rider	1 day	150	00	150	00
	Male Hustler	1 day	120	00	120	00
	Cop #1	1 day	120	00	120	00
	Cop #2	1 day	120	00	120	00
	Uncle Harry	3 days	150	00	450	00
	Hitter #1	1 day	120	00	120	00
	Hitter #2	1 day	120	00	120	00
	Mrs. Jones	1 week	400	00	400	00
	Francesca	1 week	400	00	400	00
	Gerry	1 week	400	00	400	00
	Street Speaker	1 day	120	00	120	00
	Kid #1	1 day	120	00	120	00
	Kid #2	1 day	120	00	120	00
	Head Hooker	3 days	150	00	450	00
	BUYOUTS (CONTINUED ON NEXT PAGE)		125%			
	PENSION CONTRIBUTIONS 6-1/2% of total bits				508	30
	OVERTIME ON BITS 15% of $6,800.00				1,020	00
	FITTING CHARGES					
	TOTAL BITS					

166

ACCOUNT NUMBER	DESCRIPTION	DAYS, WKS, OR QUANTITY	RATE		TOTALS	
6	Bits (continued)					
	Junior	3 days	150	00	150	00
	White Cop	1 day	120	00	120	00
	Black Cop	2 days	120	00	240	00
	Desk Cop	2 days	120	00	240	00
	Detective #1	1 week	400	00	400	00
	Detective #2	1 week	400	00	400	00
	Arresting Cop	1 day	120	00	120	00
	Bob's Mother	1 day	120	00	120	00
	Bob's Father	1 day	120	00	120	00
	Rita	1 day	120	00	120	00
	Puerto Rican #1	1 day	120	00	120	00
	Puerto Rican #2	1 day	120	00	120	00
	Puerto Rican #3	2 days	120	00	240	00

ACCOUNT NUMBER	DESCRIPTION	DAYS, WKS, OR QUANTITY	RATE		TOTALS	
7	EXTRAS					
	Rest area kids (Bl) - 2	1 day	39	15	78	30
	Rest area Mother (Bl)	1 day	39	15	39	15
	Rest Area Father (AT)	1 day	29	15	29	15
	XKE Girls(SP) - 2	1 day	74	60	149	20
	Howard Johnson Atmos. (AT) - 5	1 day	29	15	145	75
	Cop (Bl) - 7	1 day	39	15	274	05
	Cop (SP)	1 day	74	60	74	60
	Jewish Girls (AT) - 2	1 day	29	15	58	30
	Boy on Bummer (SP)	1 day	74	60	74	60
	Jewish Men (Bl) - 2	1 day	39	15	78	30
	Puerto Ricans (SP) - 6	1 day	74	50	447	00
	Hasseled Black (Bl)	1 day	39	15	39	15
	Eden Theatre Atmos. (AT) - 10	1 day	29	15	291	50
	Male Hustlers (Bl) = 3	1 day	39	15	117	45
	Street Walkers (SP) - 2	1 day	74	50	149	00
	Street Walkers (Bl) - 3	1 day	39	15	117	45
	Americana Lobby (AT) - 10	1 day	29	15	291	50
	Americana Coffee Shop (AT) - 10	1 day	29	15	291	50
	Americana SP - 2	1 day	74	50	149	00
	Whore's (Bl) - 5	4 days	39	15	783	00
	Atmos Ride to Harlem (Bl) - 7	1 day	39	15	274	05
	Passers-by Harlem (AT) - 3	1 day	29	15	87	45
	Black Johns (Bl) -4	1 day	39	15	156	60
	Car Strippers (SP) - 2	3 days	79	50	477	00
	Howard Johnson's Atmos. (AT) -6	1 day	29	15	174	90
	Howard Johnson Clerk	1 day	79	50	79	50
	Penny Pitchers (Bl) - 3	1 day	39	15	117	45
	Francine's Investment (Bl)	1 day	39	15	39	15
	Men in Dashikis - 2	1 day	39	15	78	30
	OVERTIME FOR EXTRAS 15% of $5,745.35				861	75
	FITTING FOR EXTRAS					
	SERVICE FEES FOR EXTRAS					
	ADJUSTMENTS FOR EXTRAS					
	STAND INS					
	SCHOOL TEACHER'S					
	STUNT PEOPLE					
	STUNT ADJUSTMENTS					
	BUYOUTS 75%					
	PENSION H&W CONTRIBUTIONS 5% of $6,607.10				330	37
	Misc. at (20)				583	00
	TOTAL EXTRAS				6,937	47

ACCOUNT NUMBER	DESCRIPTION	DAYS, WKS, OR QUANTITY	RATE		TOTALS	
8	**PRODUCTION STAFF SALARIES**					
	A. PRODUCTION MANAGER 12 prep/9shoot/3post	27 wks	750	00	18,000	00
	aa. Asst. Production Manager -10 prep/ ~~x UNIT MANAGER x~~ 9 shoot/3 post	20 wks	300	00	6,000	00
	B. Location Manager 7 Prep/9 prod/1 post	17 wks	200	00	3,400	00
	C. 1st ASST. DIRECTOR 4 prep/9 shoot	13 wks	600	00	7,800	00
	SEVERANCE	1 wk	600	00	600	00
	D. 2ND ASST. DIRECTOR 1 prep/9 shoot	10 wks	420	00	4,200	00
	SEVERANCE	1 wk	420	00	420	00
	E. EXTRA ASST. DIRECTORS					
	EE DGA P & W 5% 13,020 + $5.50 X 125 days				1,338	55
	F. SECRETARIES 10 prep/9 shoot/3 post	22 wks	250 (FLAT)	00	5,500	00
	G. DIALOGUE CLERK					
	H. SCRIPT CLERK 2 prep/9 prod/1 wrap	12 wks	350	00	4,500	00
	OVERTIME	100 hr	17	50	1,750	00
	~~xx DANCE DIRECTOR~~					
	I. Local #161 P & W = $5.50 X 170 days				935	00
	J. CASTING DIRECTOR & STAFF = 10% $15,265.77				1,526	50
	K. TECHNICAL ADVISOR					
	L. FIRST AID					
	M. LOCATION AUDITOR 2 prep/9 shoot/2 wrap	13 wks	350	00	4,550	00
	N. Runner 7 prep/9 prod/1 post	17 wks	140	00	2,380	00
	O. Runner 1 prep/9 prod	10 wks	100	00	1,000	00
	P. Extra Secretary 1 prep/9 prod	10 wks	100	00	1,000	00
	TOTAL PRODUCTION STAFF				64,900	05
9	**PRODUCTION OPERATING STAFF**					
	A. CAMERAMEN					
	1. 1st CAMERAMAN	~~10 wks~~	~~999~~	~~00~~	~~9,990~~	~~00~~
	2. CAMERA OPERATORS	9 wks	570	00	5,130	00
	3. FOCUS ASST. CAMERAMEN	9 wks/12 dy	350	00	3,290	00
	4. ASST. CAMERAMEN	8 wks	250	00	2,000	00
	5. CAMERA MECHANICS					
	6. COLOR DIRECTOR					
	7. STILL MAN	9 wks	400	00	3,600	00
	8. ~~STILL MAN~~ Standby 1st Cameraman	10 wks	900	00	9,000	00
	9. ~~PROCESS x CAMERA x~~ OT Standby	80 hr	22	20	1,776	00
	10. ~~ASST x x PROCESS x CAMERA x~~ OT Operator	80 hr	22	20	1,776	00
	11. ~~EXTRA CAMERA OPERATORS x~~ OT 1st Asst.	00 hr	17	50	1,750	00
	12. ~~EXTRA CAMERA ASSISTANTS x~~ OT 2nd Asst. 30% 2,000				600	00
	13. OT Still Man 20% of $3,600.00				720	00
	14% P & W 6.25 X 257 days				1,606	25
	TOTAL ACCT. 9-A				$40,248	25

ACCOUNT NUMBER	DESCRIPTION	DAYS, WKS, OR QUANTITY	RATE		TOTALS	
					$	
9	**PRODUCTION OPERATING STAFF (Contd.)**					
	B. SOUND DEPT.					
	1. MIXER	9 wk/1 dy	425	00	3,910	00
	2. RECORDER	8 wks	325	00	2,600	00
	3. BOOM MAN	8 wks	375	00	3,000	00
	4. ~~CABLEMAN~~ OT Mixer	80 hrs	21	25	1,700	00
	5. ~~CABLE BOOM MAN~~ OT Recorder	80 hrs	16	75	1,340	00
	6. ~~PA SYSTEM OPERATOR~~ OT Boom	80 hrs	18	75	1,500	00
	7. ~~DREAM OPERATOR~~ P & W $7.50 X 126 days				945	00
	8. SOUND MAINTENANCE					
	TOTAL ACCT. 9-B				$14,995	00
	C. WARDROBE DEPT.					
	1. 1ST WARDROBE DESIGNER					
	2. WARDROBE BUYER					
	3. 1ST WARDROBE GIRL 3 prep/8 prod/2 days	11 wk/2 dy	70	00 dy	3,990	00
	4. 2ND WARDROBE GIRL	5 days	65	00 dy	325	00
	5. ~~1ST WARDROBE MAN~~ OT 1st wardrobe	140 hr	17	50	2,450	00
	6. ~~2ND WARDROBE MAN~~ OT 2nd Wardrobe	10 hr	17	50	175	00
	7. TAILOR					
	8. SEAMSTRESS					
	9. EXTRA HELP					
	10. P & W 5% of $6,940.00				347	00
	TOTAL ACCT. 9-C				$ 7,287	00
	D. MAKE-UP AND HAIRDRESSING					
	1. HEAD MAKE-UP MAN	8 wk	70	00 dy	2,800	00
	2. ~~2ND MAKE-UP MAN~~ OT Make up man	100 hr	17	50	1,750	00
	3. HEAD HAIRDRESSER	1 wk	70	00 dy	350	00
	4. ~~2ND HAIRDRESSER~~ OT Hair	10 hr	17	50	175	00
	5. BODY MAKE-UP GIRL					
	6. EXTRA HELP					
	7 P & W $5.00 X 45 days				225	00
	TOTAL ACCT. 9-D				$ 5,300	00

ACCOUNT NUMBER	DESCRIPTION	DAYS, WKS. OR QUANTITY	RATE		TOTALS	
	PRODUCTION OPERATING STAFF (Contd.)					
	E. GRIP DEPT.					
	1. 1st GRIP	9 wks	75	00	3,375	00
	2. BEST BOY	9 wks	70	00	3,150	00
	3. SET OPERATION GRIPS (1)	1 wk	70	00	350	00
	4. XXXXXXXXX OT 1st Grip	100 hr	18	75	1,875	00
	5. XXXXXXXXXXXXXXXXX OT Best Boy	100 hr	17	50	1,750	00
	6 XXXXXXXXXXXXXX OT Set Op Grip	10 hr	17	50	175	00
	7. P & W $7.50 X 95 days				722	00
	TOTAL ACCT. 9-E				$11,397	00
	F. PROPERTY					
	1. HEAD PROPERTY MAN	14 wks	75	00	5,250	00
	2. 2ND PROPERTY MAN	9 wks	65	00	2,925	00
	3. XXXXXXXXXXXXX OT Head Prop	100 hr	18	75	1,875	00
	4. XXXXXXXXX OT 2nd Prop	100 hr	16	25	1,625	00
	5. XXXXXXX P & W $7.50 X 95 days				862	00
	TOTAL ACCT. 9-F				$12,537	00
	G. SET DRESSING DEPT.					
	1. XXXXXXXXXXXXXX Set Decorator	8 wks	375	00	3,000	00
	2. XXXX SET DRESSER	8 wks	375	00	3,000	00
	3. XXXXXXXX P & W $7.50 X 80 days				700	00
	4. DRAPERY MAN					
	5. ASST. DRAPERY MAN					
	6. NURSERY MAN					
	7. EXTRA LABOR					
	TOTAL ACCT. 9-G				$ 6,600	00
	H. ELECTRICAL DEPT.					
	1. GAFFER	9 wks	75	00	3,375	00
	2. BEST BOY	8 wks	70	00	2,800	00
	3. ELECTRICAL OPERATING LABOR	8 wks	65	00	2,600	00
	4. GENERATOR OPERATOR 29 Hr/3 nt		15	00	405	00
	5. XXXXXXXXXXXXXXXXXXX Extra Elec Op 27 hr nt		15	00	405	00
	6. XXXXXXXXXXXXX OT Gaffer	100 hr	18	75	1,875	00
	7. XXXXXXXXXXXXXX OT Best Boy	100 hr	17	50	1,750	00
	8. OT Elec. Op	100 hr	16	25	1,625	00
	9. P & W $7.50 X 131 days				982	50
	TOTAL ACCT. 9-H				$15,817	50

ACCOUNT NUMBER	DESCRIPTION	DAYS, WKS, OR QUANTITY	RATE		TOTALS	
9	PRODUCTION OPERATING STAFF (Contd.)					
	1. LABOR DEPT.					
	1. STANDBY LABORER					
	2. ASST. LABORERS					
	TOTAL ACCT. 9-I					
	J. SPECIAL EFFECTS					
	1. HEAD SPECIAL EFFECTS MAN					
	2. ASST. SPECIAL EFFECTS MAN					
	3. PLUMBER					
	TOTAL ACCT. 9-J					
	K. SET STANDBY OPERATORS					
	1. CARPENTER					
	TOTAL ACCT. 9-K					
	L. SET STANDBY PAINTERS 1. Painter	8 wks	70	00 day	2,800	00
	XXXXXXXX 2. OT Painter	100 hr	17	50	1,750	00
	XXXXXXXXXX 3. P & W $4.00 X40 days				160	00
	TOTAL ACCT 9L				4,710	00
	M. SET WATCHMAN					
	1. WATCHMEN					
	TOTAL ACCT. 9-M					
	N. WRANGLERS					
	1. S.P.C.A. MAN					
	2. HEAD WRANGLER					
	3. WRANGLERS					
	O. MISCELLANEOUS					
	GRAND TOTAL SET OPERATING SALARIES				$118,891	75

ACCOUNT NUMBER	DESCRIPTION	TIME		RATE				TOTAL	
10	SET CONSTRUCTION								
	A. Art Director								
	B. Asst. Art Director								
	C. Sketch Artist								
	D. Draftsman								
	E. Set Supervisor								
	F. Material & Supplies								
	G. Construction Supervisor								
	H. Miscellaneous								
		LABOR		MATERIAL					
	1 Americana Room	150	00	100	00	Loc		250	00
	2 Howard Johnson Room	75	00	100	00	Loc		175	00
	3 Police Day Room					Loc			
	4 Police Hallway					Loc			
	5 Interrogation Room	225	00	150	00	Loc		375	00
	6 Whorehouse Parlor	750	00	750	00	Loc		1,500	00
	7 Whorehouse Hall & Stair	600	00	250	00	Loc		850	00
	8 Maries Rm. Whorehouse	600	00	275	00	Loc		875	00
	9 Upstairs Bath Whorehouse	400	00	400	00	Loc		800	00
	10 Downstairs Bath W'hse.	100	00	100	00	Loc		200	00
	11 Maries Lv. Room	500	00	400	00	Loc		900	00
	12 Maries Bedroom	300	00	250	00	Loc		550	00
	13 Maries Hallway	100	00	100	00	Loc		200	00
	14 Bob's Parents' house	200	00	100	00	Loc		300	00
	15								
	16								
	17								
	18								
	19								
	20								
	21								
	22								
	23								
	24								
	25								
	26								
	27								
	28								
	29								
	30								
	31								
	32								
	33								
	34								
	35								
	36								
	37								
	38								
	39								
	Rigging Labor Grip								
	Striking								
	Backings								
	Greens								
	TOTAL SETS							$6,975	00

ACCOUNT NUMBER	DESCRIPTION	DAYS, WKS, OR QUANTITY	RATE		TOTALS	
11	SET OPERATION EXPENSES					
	A. Camera Equipment Rentals	6 wks	1,000	00	6,000	00
		3 wks	700	00	2,100	00
	B. Camera Equipment Purchases				750	00
	C. Camera Car Rentals					
	D. Camera Crane Rentals					
	E. Wardrobe Purchased				2,000	00
	F. Wardrobe Rentals				750	00
	G. Wardrobe Maintenance				750	00
	H. Grip Equipment Rented	7 wks	250	00	1,750	00
		2 wks	150	00	300	00
	I. Prop Equipment Rented	7 wks	150	00	1,050	00
		2 wks	75	00	150	00
	J. Props Purchased				1,000	00
	JJ. Prop Man's Petty Cash Exp.					
	K. Props Rented				750	00
					750	00
	L. Props - Loss & Damaged				400	00
	M. Set Dressing Rentals				2,000	00
	N. Set Dressing Purchased				2,500	00
	O. Draperies Purchased & Rented				400	00
	P. Nursery - Purchased & Rented					
	Q. Process Equipment Rentals					
	R. Make-up Purchases				500	00
	RR. Grip Purchase				500	00
	S. Hairdressing Purchases & Rentals					
	T. Electrical Equipment Rentals	7 wks	650	00	4,550	00
		2 wks	200	00	400	00
	xxxxxxxxxxxxxxxxxxxxxxxxTT Elec Extra-2 nights				1,000	00
	U. Electrical Purchases				1,500	00
	V. Electrical Power				1,000	00
	W. Rentals on Picture Cars - Trucks				4,930	00
	Planes - Wagons - Livestock, etc.					
	X. Miscellaneous Rentals & Purchases				500	00
	Y. Generator Rental - Gas & Oil					
	Z. Special Effect Purchases & Rentals					
	Total Set Operation Expense				$38,280	00

174

ACCOUNT NUMBER	DESCRIPTION	DAYS, WKS., OR QUANTITY	RATE		TOTALS	
12	CUTTING FILM LABORATORY					
	A. EDITOR 9Prod/9 post	18 wks	600	00	10,800	00
	AA. O/T	3 wks	900	00	1,800	00
	B. ASST. CUTTER 9 prod/9 post	18 wks	250	00	4,750	00
	BB. O/T	3 wks	375	00	1,125	00
	C. SOUND CUTTER					
	D. MUSIC CUTTER	2 wks	500	00	1,000	00
	DD. Local #771 P & W $10 X 46 wks				460	00
	E. NEGATIVE CUTTER	FLAT			900	00
	TOTAL LABOR					
	F. NEGATIVE ACTION RAW STOCK	150,000'	.1386		20,790	00
	G. NEGATIVE SOUND RAW STOCK	11,000'	.035		385	00
	GG. TAPE RENTAL	45-1/4"	3	10	139	50
	H. DEVELOP ACTION	150,000'	.0735		11,025	00
	HH. DEVELOP SOUND	11,000'	.035		385	00
	I. PRINT ACTION	70,000'	.1050		7,350	00
	II. PRINT SOUND Transfer Time				1,850	00
	J. MAGNASTRIPE - PRODUCTION					
	JJ. MAGNASTRIPE - SCORE & DUBBING	11,000'	.05		550	00
	K. COLOR SCENE PILOT STRIPS					
	KK. 16MM COLOR PRINTS (FROM CCO)					
	KKK. INTER-NEGATIVE					
	L. SEPARATION MASTERS					
	LL. INTER-POSITIVE	11,000'	.7658		8,424	00
	M. ANSWER PRINT	11,000'	.6697		7,367	00
	MM. COMPOSITE PRINT					
	N. FINE GRAIN PRINT					
	NN. PANCHROMATIC (FG)					
	NNN. 16MM PRINTS					
	O. FADES-DISSOLVES-DUPES & FINE GRAIN				2,100	00
	OO. REPRINTS					
	P. TITLES, MAIN & END				4,000	00
	Q. CUTTING ROOM RENTAL	18 wks.	100	00	1,800	00
	R. CODING 70 reels	70 reels	3	50	245	00
	RR. Opticals				15,000	00

ACCOUNT NUMBER	DESCRIPTION	DAYS, WKS, OR QUANTITY	RATE	TOTALS
12	CUTTING FILM LABORATORY (Contd.)			
	R. PROJECTION	70 hrs		2,100 00
	S. MOVIOLA RENTALS	22 wks		770 00
	T. REELS & LEADER			1,000 00
	U. CUTTING ROOM SUPPLIES			1,250 00
	V. STOCK SHOTS			
	W. PROCESS PLATES			
	X. SALES TAX			400 00
	~~XXX XXXXXXXX~~			
	Y. Telephone			500 00
	LABORATORY SUB-TOTAL			
	TOTAL CUTTING FILM LABORATORY			$108,265 50

ACCOUNT NUMBER	DESCRIPTION	DAYS, WKS, OR QUANTITY	RATE	TOTALS
13	MUSIC			
	A. Music Supervisor			
	B. Director			
	C. Composer			
	D. Musicians			
	E. Singers			
	F. Arrangers			
	G. Copyists			
	H. Royalties			
	I. Purchases			
	J. Miscellaneous			
	K. Instrument Rental & Cartage			
	L. Librarian			
	Total Music			11,000 00
14	SOUND			
	A. Royalties			
	B. Dubbing Room Rental	4 day	700 00	2,800 00
	C. Pre-Score Equipment Rentals			
	D. Scoring Equipment Rentals	2 hrs.	90 00 hr	1,080 00
	E. Labor for Dubbing & Etc.			
	F. Sound Equipment Rentals	8 wk	300 00	2,400 00
	G. Miscellaneous			
	H. Transfer Time	10,000'	12 50	125 00
	I. Mix	2 days	1,500 00	3,000 00
	Total Sound			9,405 00
15	TRANSPORTATION STUDIO			
	A. Labor			21,058 60
	B. Car Rentals			
	C. Truck Rentals			
	D. Bus Rentals			
	E. Car Allowance			
	F. Miscellaneous			250 00
	G. Gas & Oil, - Generator - Mileage			400 00
	H. Wranglers Cars			
	I. Livestock Transportation			
	Total Transportation			21,708 60

ACCOUNT NUMBER	DESCRIPTION	DAYS, WKS, OR QUANTITY	RATE	TOTALS	
16	**LOCATION**				
	A. TRAVELING			1,000	00
	B. HOTEL			900	00
	C. MEALS			5,450	00
	D. LOCATION SITES RENTAL			19,700	00
	E. SPECIAL EQUIPMENT			850	00
	F. CAR RENTALS (Listed under 11 W)				
	G. BUS RENTALS			700	00
	H. TRUCK RENTALS (Listed under 11 W)				
	I. SUNDRY EMPLOYEES				
	J. LOCATION OFFICE RENTAL (Listed under 16 D)				
	K. GRATUITIES				
	L. MISCELLANEOUS			750	00
	M. SCOUTING & PRE-PRODUCTION			700	00
	N. POLICE SERVICES & PERMITS			250	00
	O. CONTACT MAN			800	00
	TOTAL LOCATION			31,100	00
17	**STUDIO RENTALS**				
	A. STAGE SPACE				
	B. STREET RENTALS				
	C. TEST				
	D. VACATION ALLOWANCE (STUDIO)				
	E. SURCHARGE ON RENTALS & STUDIO CHARGES				
	F. MISCELLANEOUS EXPENSES				
	G. DRESSING ROOMS - PORTABLE				
	H. OFFICE RENTALS				
	TOTAL STUDIO RENTALS				
18	**TESTS & RETAKES**				
	A. TESTS PRIOR TO PRODUCTION			950	00
	B. TESTS DURING PRODUCTION				
	C. RETAKES AFTER PRINCIPAL PHOTOGRAPHY				
	D. PRE-PRODUCTION EXPENSE OR SHOOTING				
	TOTAL TESTS & RETAKES			950	00

ACCOUNT NUMBER	DESCRIPTION	DAYS, WKS, OR QUANTITY	RATE	TOTALS
19	**PUBLICITY**			4,000 00
	A. ADVERTISING			
	B. UNIT PUBLICITY MAN			
	C. ENTERTAINMENT			3,000 00
	D. TRADE AND NEWSPAPER SUBSCRIPTIONS			100 00
	E. PUBLICITY STILLS SALARIES			
	F. PUBLICITY STILLS SUPPLIES EQUIPMENT	8 wks	100 00	800 00
	G. PUBLICITY STILLS LAB. CHARGES			1,750 00
	H. STILL GALLERY RENTAL & EXPENSE			
	I. Trailer			
	J. PRESS PREVIEW EXPENSE			
	K. SUPPLIES POSTAGE AND EXPRESS			750 00
	L. MISCELLANEOUS			1,750 00
	TOTAL PUBLICITY			$12,150 00
20	**MISCELLANEOUS**			
	A. VACATION ALLOWANCE			
	B. RETROACTIVE WAGE CONTINGENCY			
	C. SUNDRY UNCLASSIFIED EXPENSE			
	D. COSTS IN SUSPENSE			
	E. SET COFFEE			
	F. WATER & ICE			
	TOTAL MISCELLANEOUS			
21	**INSURANCE, TAXES, LICENSE AND FEES**			
	A. CAST INSURANCE			2,000 00
	B. NEGATIVE INSURANCE			1,225 00
	C. LIFE INSURANCE			
	D. MISCELLANEOUS INSURANCE Truck Insurance			600 00
	E. COMPENSATION & PUBLIC LIABILITY INS.		%	4,400 00
	F. SOCIAL SECURITY TAX (Included in K)		%	
	G. PERSONAL PROPERTY TAX			
	H. MISCL. TAXES AND LICENSES			
	I. CODE CERTIFICATE - MPPA			2,000 00
	J. CITY TAX AND LICENSE			
	K. UNEMPLOYMENT TAX	3.5	%	4,600 00
	L. PENSION PLAN CONTRIBUTION ACTORS DIRECTORS WRITERS		%	
	M. HEALTH & WELFARE CONTRIBUTION			
	N. PENSION PLAN – CRAFTS		%	
	O. Prop/Camera Insurance			900 00
	TOTAL A/C 21			$15,725 00

178

ACCOUNT NUMBER	DESCRIPTION	DAYS, WKS, OR QUANTITY	RATE	TOTALS
22	GENERAL OVERHEAD			
	A. FLAT CHARGE			
	B. CORPORATE OVERHEAD EXPENSE			
	C. CASTING OFFICE SALARIES			
	D. ENTERTAINMENT · EXECUTIVES			1,600 00
	E. TRAVEL EXPENSE · EXECUTIVES			1,200 00
	F. OFFICE RENTAL AND EXPENSE			2,200 00
	G. AUDITOR			10,000 00
	H. TIMEKEEPER			
	I. SECRETARIES			
	J. PUBLIC RELATIONS HEAD			
	K. PUBLIC RELATIONS SECRETARY			
	L. LEGAL FEES			9,500 00
	M. OFFICE SUPPLIES			2,000 00
	N. POSTAGE · TELEPHONE & TELEGRAPH			3,500 00
	O. CUSTOMS BROKERAGE			
	P. CONTINGENCY			
	Q. GENERAL OFFICE O.H.			2,400 00
	R. FILM SHIPPING			250 00
	TOTAL GENERAL OVERHEAD			$32,650 00

Glossary

A & B Rolls—Overlapping sections of film or video tape footage wound onto separate reels to allow editing "dissolves."

A & B Windings—Specifies the way 16mm single perforation film base is wound on a reel. An "A wind" (with the emulsion toward reel hub) is generally used for contact printing; "B wind" (with base toward the reel hub) is used for camera raw stock, projection printing, and optical work.

Above-the-line—"Creative" expenses as distinguished from "technical" (below-the-line) production costs.

Academy leader—Nonprojected head section of film containing countdown cueing information in "seconds" to standards of the Academy of Motion Picture Arts and Sciences.

Acetate—Transparent plastic sheet used as an artwork surface.

A.D.—Assistant (or associate) director, detail man on set or location, before, during and after production. Also, art director.

A.F.M.—American Federation of Musicians; the music performers' union.

AFTRA—American Federation of Television and Radio Artists. One of the performing artists unions.

Ambient light—General scene lighting; light not directed at the camera subject.

Amplifier—Electrical device through which an electronic signal is strengthened.

Analyze—To "break down" sound track information in preparation for animation stand photography.

Anamorphic lens—A special lens for either photographing or projecting "wide-screen" pictures.

Animation—Giving motion or life-like appearance to still life by sequential frame-by-frame editing or exposure.

Animation stand—A device holding a camera in a fixed position above a plane on which still art may be moved frame by frame to accomplish animation photography.

.... **Announcer**—Program introducer, or commercial "pitchman."

Answer print—The first composite projection print made from a negative. Used to determine changes in color, density, and synchronization. The first acceptable A/P becomes the first release print.

Aperture—The lens opening which determines the amount of light that will pass through.

Arc light—A kind of electric light that generates light by an electric arc across two carbon electrodes rather than by a glowing filament.

A.S.A. rating—A number system rating film speed or sensitivity to light.

Aspect ratio—The numerical ratio of picture width to height.

Assembly—Putting together the shots of a film in approximately the right sequential order (also **rough cut**).

Audio—Of or concerning sound, specifically the electrical currents representing a sound program or the sound portion of a televised program.

Audio engineer—The control room engineer responsible for all sound portions of a production.

Back lighting—A technique of lighting a scene so that some of the light comes from behind the subject being shot.

Barn door—A cut-off device with two hinged doors used to control a beam of light.

B-G—Background.

Blimp—A sound-proof housing surrounding a camera which muffles or deadens camera noise so that it is not picked up by the sound-track recording microphones.

Boom—A telescoping support for a microphone or lighting fixture.

Booster light—Artificial light source which is used to augment natural daylight or exterior scenes.

Booth—A small sound-proof enclosure for voice recording.

Breakaway—Prop or set built to fall apart during violent on-camera action.

Camera—The piece of equipment, in film or video tape, that records the actual scene being shot on film or, electronically, on tape.

Camera chain—A television camera, its cables, video controls and power supply.

Camera head Pan and tilt mechanism on which a camera is mounted.

Cameraman, first—Also called director of photography. He does little actual shooting but sees that each scene is photographed in the best and most artistic way.

Camera operator—The person who actually operates the camera.

Cell—A transparent celluloid film with the drawing of a single frame used in animation. A series of cells can be photographed to give an illusion of movement.

Changing bag—A light-tight black bag with sleeves through which a person can put his arms to transfer raw, unexposed film from cans into magazines and vice versa.

Chroma key—A matting process whereby what is to be matted is shot against a blue (or red or green) background with a color camera. In optically making the matte, blue (or red or green) becomes invisible and the background seen from a second camera comes through. This system is used for matting people or objects over another scene.

Cinex strip—A strip of film with one frame of a scene printed with different light intensities so that the film laboratory can judge the proper printing exposure.

Clapstick—A pair of hinged sticks which are banged together in view of the camera at the beginning of a take. In editing, the sound of the sticks and the picture frame of them coming together aligns the picture and track for synchronization.

Composite master—First completed end-product of sound and picture, wherein all elements and effects are included.

Contact printing—A method of printing in which the raw stock is held in contact with the film to be copied.

Control board—Electronic and manual operating panel through which video and audio elements are switched and controlled. Sometimes referred to only as "switcher" or console.

Control room—Room or enclosure where all elements of a TV production are controlled; i.e., video and audio switching.

Cookie—Object used to cast a shadow on scenic elements.

Crab dolly—A dolly with front and back wheels that can be turned parallel to each other in any direction.

Cranes—Large camera mounts which permit smooth mechanical vertical and horizontal camera movements.

Crawl—A device that permits titles to move vertically past a camera lens. Usually motor driven for smooth operation.

CRI—Color Reversal Internegative. 35mm or 16mm duplicate color negative made by a direct reversal process from a negative.

Cue track—That portion of video tape on which signals are recorded for editing purposes.

Cyc—Short for cyclorama, a smooth continuous piece of material stretched taut and used as background to give the illusion of infinity.

Dailies or rushes—The first (uncorrected) print of the camera negative which is cut up to make the workprint.

Definition—Also called resolution. The fidelity with which detail is reproduced by a television receiver.

DGA—Directors Guild of America.

Diffusion lens—A camera lens designed to give a soft or blurred image around the edges of the picture.

Dimmers—Controls used for adjusting light intensity.

Documentary—A loose kind of film story dealing more with present reality than fiction or history. Objective rather than subjective.

Dolly—A wheeled camera mount.

Dolly tracks—Metal tracks in which dolly wheels are placed to permit smooth camera moves.

Double head—Two camera heads mounted at right angles in order to allow double pan and tilt.

Double system sound—The preferred system of sound recording wherein the sound is recorded on tape during photography, entirely separate from the picture.

Dubbing—Duplicating video tape or inserting new audio into video.

Editec—A device used to program frame-by-frame electronic editing.

Effects—Scene changes other than direct cuts; i.e., dissolves, fades, wipes, etc. Also sound effects, other than speech or music.

Effects filter—An optical filter used over the camera lens to change the appearance of the scene being photographed.

Effects track—The audio tape which includes all sound in proper order and blend to be used in a production.

Electrician—One of the crew responsible for the placing and adjustment of the lights and also responsible for arranging for the supply of electricity to run them.

Electronic editing—That process where different picture and sound elements (live or prerecorded) are edited together without physically cutting the tape. Done by electronic pulses.

Elements—Individual portions of a total production; i.o., sound, picture, M & E tracks, announce track, etc.

Erase head—The device on a tape recorder that erases the tape as the tape passes over it. It is always positioned ahead of the record head.

ESU—Engineering Set Up.

Fast motion—When a scene is photographed at less than the standard rate of 24 frames per second and subsequently projected at 24 fps, the resulting action on the screen appears to be faster than normal.

Fearless Dolly—Brand name of a widely used camera mount permitting smooth camera moves in or out. Will not crab.

Fill lighting—Supplements general illumination for the particular effects desired.

Film chain—A film projector, its related camera, cables, monitor, controls, and power supply.

Film transfer—A film copy of a video taped production (also called a kine or kinescope recording).

Filter—Glass or gelatin screens placed in front of the camera lens to compensate for various different photographic conditions and to give various effects.

Fine grain (in color, interpositive)—A positive copy of a negative used only for reproduction of another negative.

First generation—The original or master, not a copy.

Fishpole—A hand-held mike boom.

Flat—A piece of scenery usually constructed of canvas and wood on which a scene is painted.

Flip card—A title card fashioned with grommet holes and mounted on rings so that it may be dropped in front of a camera.

Flip stand—Stand for holding title cards.

Floor manager—Also stage manager. Executes director's orders on the studio floor. Responsible for setup of physical parts of the scene and directing talent while on-camera.

FPS—Frames per second; the number of pictures produced every second as the film passes in front of the camera aperture.

Friction head—A device mounted on the tripod that permits the camera to be swung manually either horizontally or vertically.

Front lighting—The simplest form of lighting wherein the main source of light for a scene is in front of the subject being photographed.

Gaffer—An electrician.

Geared head—Camera mount where movement is controlled by two hand cranks.

Generator—A self-powered piece of equipment that produces stable electrical power. Often used on location or remote shooting as a source of power when regular power is not available.

Gobo—A cutout of cardboard, wood or other material placed in front of a camera shot. Miniature doors are often made as gobos so the camera may move through, giving the appearance of an actual door. Also used to control light distribution.

Grip—A stagehand or man who moves scenery, dollies, etc.

Head—The device on a tape recorder, audio or video, that causes magnetic impulses to be placed on the tape, recording picture or sound.

Head, camera—Camera mount.

High hat—A short mount to add height to the camera.

IATSE—International Alliance of Theatrical Stage Employees and Motion Picture Machine Operators of the United States and Canada. One of the three major engineering unions in broadcasting.

IBEW—International Brotherhood of Electrical Workers. One of the three major engineering unions in broadcasting.

Idiot cards—Cue cards on which a script is written for a performer.

In the can—A term describing a scene or program which has been completed; "it's finished."

Inky-dink—A miniature incandescent studio lamp used for providing a small spot of light.

Insert stage—A small stage for shooting m.o.s. scenes such as product shots.

Interiors—Indoor scenes.

Interlock—The ability to synchronize two or more sound and-or picture sources together.

Interpositive—An intermediate positive stock that is kept by the lab as protection if the negative is damaged in printing. A new negative can then be made from the IP.

Iris—Optically, the adjustable mask which limits the amount of light allowed to enter a lens. Its adjustment controls both the amount of light used to excite television electronics and also the depth of field.

Key light—Usually the stronger of the lights focused on a subject for modeling effect.

Kine—A film recording of a television picture, live or tape. Short for kinescope.

LD—Lighting director.

Leader—A timed visual used at the beginnings of scenes for cue purposes.

Lighting—The art of illuminating a scene to be photographed.

Live recording—Recording of actual sounds as they occur as contrasted to prerecorded and postrecorded sounds.

Location—Any shooting site remote from a studio.

M & E track—Music and effects recording on separate stock.

Mag track—Magnetically recorded audio on film stock.

Magazine—Film container on a camera.

Master—The original video tape recording of a finished product.

Matte—The imposition of a scene or title over another scene. In matting, the background scene does not bleed or show through.

Mix—To blend several elements, audio and-or visual, to make a composite recording.

Mobile unit—A truck, van or trailer containing cameras, control gear, related cables, power, control room and video tape recorders, completely self-contained and used for location shooting.

M.O.S.—To shoot a scene silent. Said to have originated years ago when a certain German director used to scream "Ve vill shoot dis next scene mit out sound." Since shortened to M.O.S.

Moviola—A film editing device which runs picture and-or sound film forward or reverse at any speed.

NABET—National Association of Broadcast Employees and Technicians, one of three major television engineering unions.

Negative—The negative exposed by the camera.

Nemo—Term meaning "remote pick up." Came about through a typographical error. In shortening "remote" to "remo," a typist typed "nemo" instead.

Night filter—A special effects filter used on the camera which modifies sunlight in such a way that scenes can be photographed in the daytime to simulate night.

One-light workprint—An inexpensive print made with the printer set at only one level of light intensity without regard to variations of exposure between the individual scenes.

Optical blowup—Process of enlarging part of a scene already on film.

Optical sound—Permanent sound achieved with light variations (modulations) photographically placed on the side of a film. As light shines through the modulations, it introduces variations in light which are translated to sound.

Opticals—Any variations added to the picture achieved during or after shooting. If multiple cameras are used in shooting video tape, optical effects can be accomplished through a control board during the taping process. In film, they are the various special effects put in after the workprint has been edited.

Optics—Refers to visual properties of lenses.

Original—Refers to the film actually exposed in the camera, whether negative or reversal.

Original picture negative—Negative film exposed in a camera and processed to produce a negative image of the original subject.

Outtakes—Any scene photographed which is not used in the final production. (Also **trims**).

Oxberry—The most often used and versatile animation stand.

PA—Production assistant.

Pan head—A mount for a camera that permits horizontal and vertical movement.

Picture duplicate negative—A "dupe" negative.

Pop on—A title or object that is inserted into a scene instantly rather than faded in.

Post production—All work done after shooting. Examples: editing, mixing, optical effects, timing, etc.

Printer—A machine reproducing a print from a negative.

Print generations—The number of print stages made from original picture negative to final release print. Picture gets grainier with each successive generation.

Printing—The operation of exposing raw stock to the processed image of another film; taking a picture of a picture.

Prism—A means of optically controlling light direction.

Processing—A generic term applied to the total operation necessary to produce a permanent visible image on exposed film.

Producer—The individual responsible for all production details.

Production unit—The complete team that photographs the scenes and records the sound for film and video tape production.

Prop—A theatrically derived abbreviation for property; any portable article on the set.

Raw stock—New, yet to be used, stock (film or tape).

Rear projection—Scenes are projected onto the rear translucent screen from the opposite side from where performers are being filmed. Gives the illusion of being "on location" right in the studio.

Recordist—The person who is responsible for recording the sound and operating the sound equipment.

Release negative—The composite negative containing all music, dialogue, sound effects, opticals, titles, etc., for printing release prints.

Release print—A complete composite print ready for distribution and projection.

Remote unit—Same as "mobile unit."

Reversal film—Film which produces a positive image instead of a negative one.

Reversal print—A reversal-type film that has been exposed to a positive film image, processed by the reversal process, producing a positive image.

Rewinds—Pedestals with square spindles mounted on an editing table for rewinding film. Some are hand cranked and some motor driven.

Room tone-room noise—A kind of tone quality in sound recording which is characterized by the "boominess" which sometimes occurs when the recording is done in a small room. Also, gives you the necessary background noise for your production if sound and picture are recorded at different times.

Rough cut—The first edited version of the film in which the scenes generally follow each other in their intended order, although they have not yet been trimmed in length for pacing or mood.

Rushes—The first (uncorrected) print of the camera negative which is cut to make the work print (same as dailies).

S.A.G.—Screen Actors Guild.

Scenic designer—Art director who designs sets.

Scoop—A special kind of studio light without a lens.

Scratch track—A rough voice recording used as an audio timing guide in shooting or editing.

Scrim—A translucent diffuser placed over a light to soften its intensity.

Script supervisor—A person who notes the details and timings of each take. These notations are given to the editor as a guide.

Second generation—A tape copy of the master tape. Also, in film, the second copy used for duping.

Set—The basic background or area for a production.

SFX—Sound effects.

Single system—Where both audio and video are recorded on the same piece of stock. Newsreel photography and video tape are single systems.

Slate—A placard identifying the scene which is photographed at its beginning.

Slop print—After an optical negative is made, it is printed quickly without the sound track or corrections and screened to see if the opticals are correct.

SMPTE—Society of Motion Picture and Television Engineers. Society that sets standards for the film industry.

Special effects—Any visual or audio effects, other than the standard opticals, such as mattes, wipes, split screen, etc.

Split screen—Two different scenes on the screen at the same time.

Stock footage—Footage from film libraries that is available (purchase or rental) for use in other films.

Stop motion—Freezing a single frame of action into a still picture for as long as desired.

Strike (the set)—To tear down a scene in the studio; i.e., "strike the set."

Studio control room—The room or location where the monitoring and switching equipment is placed for the direction and control of a television program.

Super—Superimposition of one scene over the other.

Switching—Choosing a single picture from between two or more cameras.

Sync—Synchronization of sound and picture.

Sync generator—Generates the reference pulses fed to TV cameras and recorders.

TD—Technical director; engineer who is in charge of the engineering crew and equipment and who physically operates the video control board.

Telecine—The film projection room of a broadcast station or video tape production house.

Track—The portion of a film that contains the sound recording.

Triangle—A folding, adjustable, three-armed rack that lies flat on the ground and serves as the foundation for a camera tripod.

Tripod—A three-legged support for a camera.

Video—Of or pertaining to sight; specifically, those electrical currents representing the elements of a television picture.

Video engineer—The engineer who controls and adjusts the picture quality of a television camera.

Video tape—Material two inches wide, on which electronic impulses may be recorded magnetically and then reproduced into a picture. The picture and sound are both recorded on the same continuous piece of stock. Broadcast quality is 2 inches wide; other sizes available are 1 inch, ½ inch, and ¾ inch.

Vidicon—A television camera tube of moderate sensitivity, adequate for most instructional broadcast requirements (black-and-white only).

Vinton pan & tilt head—A type of camera mount permitting extremely smooth pan and tilt motions.

Voice-over—A spoken message delivered off-camera as a narrative to television scenes.

VTR—An abbreviation for Video Tape Recorder.

Wild footage—Picture or sound that are recorded, without benefit of a script.

Wild track—Nonsynchronous sound.

Workprint—The edited dailies, with all opticals, fades, dissolves so indicated in grease pencil on the actual print.

Zoom lens—A lens with a variable focal length that permits in or out motion without physical movement of the camera or change of lens.

Index

A

Accident insurance	140
Administrative personnel	144
Agents	104
Animal rentals	137
Animation	129,132
—stand effects	133
—stand photography	132
Artwork	110
Audio tape	71

B

Budget checklists	19
Budget considerations	104
Budgets, sample	150

C

Cameras & accessories	23
Cast insurance	140
Casting director, staff	104
Casting services, outside	103
Charges, laboratory	10,73
Charges, sound	10
Checklists, budget	19
Comprehensive general-auto liability	138
Cost cutting	108
Cue cards	111

D

Damage, third-party property	140
Developing	73
Differential, night	105
Director, staff casting	104

E

Editing	11,122,148
—film	124
Editor, hiring	128
Effects animation stand	133
—optical	129
—sound	88
—special	137

Equipment

Equipment	22,147
—costs	9
—insurance	139
Errors and omissions insurance	140
Extra expense insurance	139

F

Fees, writer's	136
Film	69
—editing	124
—equipment	22
Final processes	75
Fittings	105
Flight insurance	106
Food	113

H

Hiring an editor	128
Holiday work	106

I

Insurance	138
—accident	140
—cast	140
—equipment	139
—errors and omissions	140
—extra	139
—flight	106
—negative	139
—weather	140

L

Laboratory charges	10,73
Lighting	29
Location considerations	120
—expenses	113,148
—release fees	116
—shooting	18
Lodging	114

M

Make-up tests	105

Meal penalties 105
Messenger services 143
Mileage 115
Mixing 89
Music 07

N

Narration 89
Negative insurance 139
Night differential 105
Nonunion production 145

O

Office personnel 144
Office supplies 143
Optical effects 129
Outside casting services 103
Overhead 12,107,142,147

P

Penalties, meal 105
Per diem 106
Personnel 9
—production 92
—technical 92
Postproduction costs 11
Printing 74
Production
—do-it-yourself 107
—nonunion 145
—personnel 92,149
Property damage,
    third-party 140
Props 139

R

Ratio, shooting 71
Raw stock 9,68
Recording 85
—sound 26
Rehearsals 105
Rentals
—animal 137
—vehicle 114

S

Sample budgets 150
Saturday work 106
Scenic
—considerations 10
—elements 109,148

Session fees 104
Set 139
—building 109
Shipping 115
Shooting
—location 18
—ratio 71
Sound
—charges 10
—costs 85
—effects 88
—recording 26
Special effects 137
Staff casting director 104
Stock, raw 9,68
Studio specifications 14
Sunday work 106
Survey 147,148

T

Talent 102
Tape
—audio 71
—video 31,68,122
Technical personnel 92,149
Telephone 142
Teleprompter 111
Third-party property
    damage 140
Transfers 86
Transportation 13
Travel time 105,116
Traveling expenses 106
Trucking 112

U

Union pension and
    welfare contributions 106

V

Vehicle rentals 114
Video tape 31,68,122

W

Wardrobe 105,111,139
—tests 105
Weather
—days 106
—insurance 140
Workmen's compensation 138
Writer's fees 136